Death to the Dictator!

WITNESSING IRAN'S ELECTION AND THE CRIPPLING OF THE ISLAMIC REPUBLIC

AFSANEH MOQADAM

THE BODLEY HEAD
LONDON

Published by The Bodley Head 2010

2 4 6 8 10 9 7 5 3 1

First published in Great Britain in 2010 by
The Bodley Head
Random House, 20 Vauxhall Bridge Road
London SW1V 2SA

www.bodleyhead.co.uk
www.rbooks.co.uk

Addresses for companies within The Random House Group Limited can be found at:
www.randomhouse.co.uk/offices.htm

The Random House Group Limited Reg. No. 954009

A CIP catalogue record for this book is available from the British Library.

ISBN 9781847921468

The Random House Group Limited supports The Forest Stewardship
Council (FSC), the leading international forest certification organisation. All our titles
that are printed on Greenpeace approved FSC certified paper carry the FSC logo. Our
paper procurement policy can be found at www.rbooks.co.uk/environment

Mixed Sources

Product group from well-managed
forests and other controlled sources
www.fsc.org Cert no. TT-COC-2139
© 1996 Forest Stewardship Council

Typeset by Palimpsest Book Production Limited, Grangemouth, Stirlingshire
Printed and bound in Great Britain by Clays Ltd., St Ives PLC

Author's Note

The characters in this book have been given pseudonyms in order to protect them.

They were going to print Ahmadinejad's face on a stamp, but the people were confused. They didn't know which side to spit on.

Prologue

Mohsen was freed at 2 a.m. on August 29, 2009. They flung him out of a moving van at one of the big roundabouts south of Tehran, wearing a pair of pyjama pants and the T-shirt he was arrested in. He picked himself up and stood at the side of the road until an off-duty taxi-driver stopped and asked him if he needed help. Mohsen went back to the taxi-driver's house, where he was given a shower and some clean clothes. Then he asked to be taken home.

It was past 4 a.m. when Mohsen finally got back to the apartment, and the instinctive reaction of his parents to the sound of the buzzer was to assume it was the Intelligence Ministry again. After deliberating with his wife, Mohsen's father asked who it was.

When the elevator door opened and the taxi-driver emerged with Mohsen, Mr and Mrs Abbaspour barely recognised their son. He was emaciated and grey. He stared at them through lifeless eyes. The taxi-driver refused to take any money. Wiping a tear, he got back into the elevator.

After entering the apartment, Mohsen didn't say much. His mother fussed and stroked his hair and her questions came rushing out, but Mr Abbaspour calmed her, saying, 'There will be plenty of time for questions. Let the boy rest a while.' Mohsen had tea and dates while leaning against the kitchen counter. Then he yawned and his mother took him into his room, which she had tidied immaculately, and she had to run out again in order not to sob in front of him. After composing herself, she came back in and asked if he wanted her to undress him. Mohsen got into bed still wearing the taxi-driver's clothes and immediately fell asleep.

Mohsen's parents did not sleep for the rest of that night. Mrs Abbaspour fluttered around the place, arranging things neatly, getting the breakfast things ready, soaking kidney beans for a *ghormeh sabzi* – a herb stew. 'He loves his mother's *ghormeh sabzi*,' she said, but her husband warned, 'Massi! Don't expect too much of him. And don't tell anyone he's out until he's ready. Do you understand?'

The following day Mohsen was quiet. He slept a lot and said very little. He preferred to lie on the sofa, on his side, rather than sit, and watch DVDs. He didn't touch his mother's *ghormeh sabzi*, though she kept it simmering all day.

Mrs Abbaspour poured her love into Mohsen's feet. The soles of his feet were red and black and covered in welts. Mrs Abbaspour prepared footbaths and balms. She went out to buy him a pair of soft slippers. She clipped his filthy toenails as he watched his DVDs. Every now and then she would be overcome with emotion and murmur, 'I am your sacrifice!' Out in the corridor she whispered to her husband, 'He lost three toenails. Two of his teeth are wobbly. Have you seen the state of his wrists?' Then she clapped her hand over her mouth and said, 'Let them die, please God. Please God, let them all die.'

The next day Mohsen told his mother that he needed to go to a doctor. Not the family doctor. He wanted a doctor he didn't know. After lunch Mrs Abbaspour sent her husband down to the basement parking lot. 'No one down here,' he whispered into his cellphone, before sending the elevator up to the third floor. 'You can come down.'

Mrs Abbaspour drove her son to a hospital quite far from home, where several doctors had afternoon surgeries. Mohsen hobbled into the doctor's room and stayed there for a very long time. When he and the doctor came out, Mrs Abbaspour saw that the doctor's eyes were red. Mohsen crossed the waiting hall to have some water from a drinking fountain, and the doctor said to her, 'I need to speak to you. Come and see me after my surgery closes.'

That evening Mrs Abbaspour left Mohsen with his father and went back to the hospital. The surgery was over and the doctor was getting ready to go home. He invited Mrs Abbaspour into his office and they sat in silence as he composed himself. At length, looking at the picture on the wall behind her, he asked Mrs Abbaspour what she knew of Mohsen's incarceration.

'Only what I see,' she replied.

'Mrs Abbaspour,' the doctor went on, 'I'm afraid your son has suffered a great deal. At present he doesn't want to talk, and this is entirely natural. It was with the greatest difficulty that I persuaded him to agree that I should speak with you.'

Mrs Abbaspour wept silently as the doctor told her that Mohsen had been raped while he was in custody. Not once: many times. He had been terribly and repeatedly beaten. The indications were that Mohsen's internal bleeding had stopped, but there remained a risk of infection around the anus, where the tissue had been severely torn. 'He was stitched up while in custody,' the doctor went on, 'but I removed the stitches when I saw him this afternoon, and this should make him more comfortable. I disinfected him thoroughly, but he is still sore and should observe a strict regime of potty-baths. And of course there are his antibiotics.' The doctor handed Mrs Abbaspour a prescription.

He asked Mrs Abbaspour to bring Mohsen to see him again in a couple of days. He ordered an MRI scan to determine the extent of the injuries in the rectum. 'It's very important that he continues to check his urine and faeces for blood, as any recurrence of the internal bleeding would be dangerous.' He paused. 'I'm afraid it's going to be painful for him to defecate.'

Mrs Abbaspour was sobbing freely now – sobbing for her son, sobbing for herself, sitting and being told these things by a stranger.

When it was time to go, the doctor said, 'I advise you to monitor Mohsen's psychological condition closely, even after he improves physically. I have heard of other young people who have suffered like this and have not been able to face life after their experiences – the most recent instance came to my attention yesterday.'

As she left the room, the doctor said, 'May God help you, Mrs Abbaspour.'

Little by little, over the next couple of weeks, Mohsen got stronger. His wounds began to heal and his appetite returned.

Mrs Abbaspour shielded her son from the other stories and reports that were coming out of the detention centres. She kept her husband's newspapers out of sight and insisted that he watch TV only when Mohsen was in his room.

Mohsen was only vaguely aware of the big show trial of opposition politicians and their supporters that had gotten under way. He only learned much later of the dozens of unmarked graves that had recently been dug at the main Tehran cemetery – the graves of other protesters and other detainees, who were not so lucky.

Mohsen was physically present, nothing more. His gaze was neutral. He didn't play his *setar* or read his books of poetry. On the rare occasions when he went out, to see the doctor or take a medical test, his mother went to elaborate lengths to ensure they weren't seen by friends or acquaintances. Mohsen would scream at night and his mother would rush in and cradle him. She tried not to leave him alone. To neighbours and family members who telephoned or rang the buzzer as they passed, she said that she had come down with something and wouldn't see anyone until she was better. She sent her husband out to do the shopping.

One day Mrs Abbaspour could stand it no longer and asked Mohsen to tell her what had happened when he was inside, and he shouted at her and she got upset. She would have liked to turn to someone – a wise older member of the family, a mullah, a shrink – but Mohsen forbade her from doing so. Again and again Mr Abbaspour repeated that time is a great healer, but he didn't believe his own words. He knew people from the Left who were still soft in the head even though they were released twenty-five years ago.

About two weeks after Mohsen was released, Shadi rang the buzzer. Shadi had done this several times since the news spread that Mohsen had been arrested, but she had never received an answer. She had asked around and learned that Mohsen's family had not gone away. She had assumed they were screening visitors.

On this occasion, as she waited, the door of the apartment block opened and Mrs Abbaspour came outside. She was going to the drugstore for Mohsen and didn't recognise Shadi standing on the step. But Shadi recognised her and introduced herself as a friend of Mohsen.

In normal circumstances Mrs Abbaspour would have felt affronted at being approached in this way, by a woman whose relationship with Mohsen was ambiguous. But Mrs Abbaspour felt terribly alone, and Shadi's face was persuasive as well as kind. When Shadi asked if there was news of Mohsen, Mrs Abbaspour started crying – there on the step, tears rolling down her cheeks. Shadi thought Mohsen's mother was crying because she had no news. She was astonished when Mrs Abbaspour mumbled, 'He's at home right now.'

The two women entered the apartment and Shadi knocked on Mohsen's door. There was no answer, so she said, 'It's me: Shadi. Can I come in?' She opened the door. Mohsen was lying on his bed. She shut the door behind her. '*Salaam*, Mohsen.'

After a while of sitting with Shadi and hearing some bits of news, Mohsen raised his hand to shush her. He wanted to speak, but couldn't. He rocked on his haunches and he cried and cried. Each time he opened his mouth to say something, he was prevented by a fresh spasm. He began to convulse. He looked around wildly. He went down on his knees.

Mrs Abbaspour was standing on the other side of the closed door. When she heard Mohsen sobbing, she was tempted to burst in and demand that Shadi stop tormenting her son and leave the house. Then she heared Shadi murmuring and Mohsen's breathing became more regular, and eventually he had used up all his sobbing for now.

Mrs Abbaspour went softly to the kitchen and came back with tea and sweets. Shadi opened the door at her knock, smiled encouragingly and took the tray. Shadi mouthed the word 'alone!' and Mrs Abbaspour nodded. She said, 'I'm going out for a few minutes.' Shadi and Mohsen heard the door of the apartment slam shut and drank their tea in silence.

'Tell,' she said, stroking his hand.

'I can't remember a lot,' he replied.

'It doesn't matter. Just tell.'

1

It's June 8, 2009, a few days before the election, and Mohsen Abbaspour is walking down the hill towards Vali-ye Asr Street. The oriental planes bowing over the street were planted by Reza, the last Shah's father. Reza was a doer. He did development and railways and a modern army. He did horse-whippings and larceny. Now there is Mahmoud Ahmadinejad. He does Big Lies and nuclear centrifuges. He thinks he was crowned with a divine halo.

For the past four years Mohsen has laughed at him. He and his friends made up jokes about him and sent them by text to each other. The nation's children laughed because Ahmadinejad looked like the monkey on the Cheetos packet. But inside they were sad, because they were ashamed. They were ashamed that he represented Iran.

The Iranians are a cultured people, a people with a past. Did they not give the world Avicenna, squinches, the divine right of kings? Did Cyrus the Great not author the first declaration of human rights? Wasn't Goethe enthralled by the verse of Hafez, Emerson by that of Sa'adi? Now Iran is represented by a midget with lethal, half-asleep eyes. He prances on the international stage – with Hugo Chávez and the President of Belarus. If he is not a mass murderer, not yet, this is because he is not alone at the top of Iran's pyramid of power. Make no mistake: he wouldn't hesitate.

Ahmadinejad must share with Ali Khamenei. Ayatollah Ali Khamenei is the Supreme Leader of Iran. He should not be mistaken for Khomeini, even if their names sound alike. Khomeini was the father of the revolution. Love him or hate him (some did both), you couldn't but admire his courage and integrity. Such was his presence and authority that the people called him the Imam. When Khomeini died in 1989, there was no obvious replacement. Khamenei got the nod, a startled apparatchik who admitted to his unfitness for the job of being God's representative on Earth.

On the contrary, the oilers and greasers whispered, the position suits you very well. You are truly an historical eminence, the merest of steps away from divinity. In time, Khamenei started to like the sound of all this. Now he inclines his head graciously when they say that obedience to Khamenei is as important as saying your prayers. Don't forget to smile, your Grace the Ayatollah! The posters of the Supreme Leader used to show him in a bad mood. Now they show him grinning, above reminders that this year is the year of reforming patterns of consumption.

Khomeini never smiled. He was too big, too awesome, to smile.

In theory Khamenei and his president are great friends. Khamenei helped Ahmadinejad come to power in 2005. Did Ahmadinejad show his gratitude? Like hell he did. Ahmadinejad is dissimilar to Khamenei. He doesn't lack confidence, doesn't need puffing up. Ahmadinejad believes he enjoys the favour of the Hidden Imam, whose re-emergence among us will begin a period of justice and truth, and the Hidden Imam, as everyone knows, is closer to God than the Supreme Leader is. During his first term, Ahmadinejad professed undying loyalty to Khamenei, but in fact did his own thing. Sometimes Khamenei approved, sometimes he didn't. To Ahmadinejad, crowned by his halo, it didn't much matter either way.

Iran's electorate knows they will never get the chance to sack his Grace the Ayatollah. The constitution doesn't give them that privilege. Even if they could, there's a strong chance they would choose not to, for where's the guarantee they wouldn't get someone worse? There are rumours, which periodically gust and die, to the effect that Khamenei suffers from an advanced form of cancer, or that he and the opium pipe are inseparable. Then comes another, contradictory rumour; Khamenei's as fit as a fiddle. So the people don't occupy themselves with thoughts of dumping Khamenei. The Supreme Leader is supreme for life. Amen.

But, the president . . . that's a different matter. The constitution allows the people to vote for a president and a parliament. Granted, this only happens after the candidates have been vetted by the Council of Guardians for their adherence to Islamic tenets and their aptitude for office. This means that the vast majority of candidates get weeded out, but a certain number get through, and a certain number of this certain number are reformists.

Back at the beginning, the reformists were disciples of Khomeini. They were hostage-takers and, in the manner of ideologues everywhere, advocates of death for anyone who didn't agree with them. Now they have changed. They are democrats, supporters of women's rights, they love music and books. They won't say sorry for the past; Iranians don't really go in for apologies. But they are definitely preferable to the hardliners, the conservatives – the 'Principalists', in their own jargon – who swarm around Khamenei and Ahmadinejad. Come election time, the only question for Mohsen is whether to vote for the reformists, or not at all.

Mohsen has been debating this question with his friend Amin. Khamenei and some of the other mullahs emphasise the importance of a really high turnout. The enemy, Khamenei says, is working night and day to ensure this won't happen. Everyone agrees that a high turnout would be read as a popular legitimisation of the Islamic Republic. Mohsen and Amin could live with this, so long as someone better than Ahmadinejad gets in. They don't like the Islamic Republic, this jackbooted kleptocracy with its chorus-line of seers and charlatans. They despise its bullying, its dirty fingers touching their beliefs and private lives. But they are prepared to accept it on condition that it reforms itself, adheres to those bits of the constitution that promise freedom, and repairs the country's terribly damaged image abroad.

The reason is simple. Mohsen and Amin don't want another revolution. Their parents made the last one and look where that got them. Mohsen and Amin don't want bloodshed and upheaval. They want reform. Perhaps they are yellow, these children of the revolution. Or perhaps they are smart.

There was a time before Ahmadinejad, during Iran's first and only reformist government, when the bearer of an Iranian passport was not automatically regarded with suspicion and fear. The president was Muhammad Khatami, and he was a good-looking, well-dressed mullah. No matter that Khatami was ineffective at home, or that the conservatives wouldn't let him carry out his reforms; he repaired Iran's image abroad, with his white teeth and his call for a dialogue among civilisations. During his tenure it happened, every now and then, that an Iranian travelling to Europe was not treated as the carrier of a dangerous bacillus.

'Ah,' the customs official smiled, 'Khatami! Nice man! Nice hat!'

Since Ahmadinejad came to power and got the Israelis' backs up, things have changed again, the other way. Iran's fellow pariahs, the Iraqis, the Libyans and the Syrians, have been let back into the gang – they are now acceptable members of the community of nations. The North Koreans don't often let their citizens out; the passport issue doesn't arise. That leaves Iran.

The Iranian passport is the least-cool passport in circulation today. When it falls with a slap on the immigration-hall counter, it elicits the same reaction as a warm, dead bird. Nostrils wrinkle.

Get rid of it!

Earlier this year Mohsen decided to go for a short trip. It would be his first trip abroad. He would go to Italy, where his cousin lives. This cousin has a job. He shares a small apartment with several other Iranians.

Italy, the home of Dante, Levi, Fo. The home of hot Italian

girls. Mohsen had an invitation. He would go to the embassy and get a visa.

One morning Mohsen joined a forlorn ribbon of people. They were respectable people, giants in their fields, some of them, but they held themselves shoddy and bent. They knew, all of them, what would happen inside. They would be insulted and humiliated by the visa officer who interviewed them. This officer would not be Italian. She would be an Iranian, a member of the embassy's local staff, a quisling whose long years at the embassy had taught her to regard her own people with warm, dead-bird disdain. If, by any chance, she did not humiliate them, they would feel pathetically grateful.

In his hands Mohsen had his forms (in triplicate), his photographs, his fee, and a deed to his parents' apartment made out in his name, forged that very morning – evidence that he would not do a runner in Italy and become an illegal. Sweating, feeling sick, he stood before the bulletproof glass that walled him from the quisling, and the noise of his anger rose in his ears as he tried to explain away some alleged error in the forms that he had filled out in triplicate, an error that rendered them utterly worthless, worse than worthless; and then, as he pleaded and stammered, the quisling started examining the nail she had broken that very morning, tilting it in the halogen light.

'Rejected.'

Mohsen and Amin were born in the war. Saddam was firing Scuds at Tehran, and anyone who could get away, anyone with relations outside Tehran, fled the game of chance. Mohsen's father was a junior government official. He told Mohsen's mother to take the boy and get away to her sister's place near Tabriz, but she refused to leave him. Amin's father had walked on a mine at the front and was laid up. He needed medical attention and couldn't go far from the hospital. Amin and Mohsen were both born in Tehran after the city had emptied. It was the height of the air war, and some of their earliest memories are of sheltering underground with their respective families, in an old cistern.

Another of the neighbours had a good voice and she sang to keep spirits up – love songs by Marzieh, Delkash, Ghamar.

Mohsen and Amin grew up in the same street. In those days, before the construction boom, there were few apartment blocks, just small houses with small yards. Mohsen and Amin climbed over the walls and stole from the yards – quinces, mulberries white and black, persimmons. Amin and Mohsen went through school together. They played truant, went to the cinema, smoked cigarettes, read anything they could get their hands on. They tried alcohol, marijuana. Mohsen wanted to buy some crack, but Amin persuaded him to come camping and he forgot about it. They grew up, did their military service, were admitted to university. Amin got in to study computers, and Mohsen, Persian literature.

'What are you going to do with a degree in Persian literature?' his father demanded. 'It won't help you get a job.' After a couple of years he bowed to his father's pressure and changed to engineering, but he hated engineering and spent his time buried in politics and literature. He read Soroush, Popper, Paine. He got hold of some banned copies of Solzhenitsyn. Mohsen's father had been a Communist at the time of the revolution, a member of the outlawed *Tudeh* Party; he had saved himself by becoming a Khomeinist, growing a beard and giving up the booze, but many of his friends had been to jail. Don't get too close to politics, he told Mohsen. Remember Icarus in the old Greek story; he flew too close to the sun and his wings melted.

Mohsen was thirteen when Khatami presented himself for election. He and Amin were too young to vote, but they watched with excitement all the same. Khatami represented New Religious Thought and his opponent represented More of the Same. Khatami was an ally of Soroush, and Soroush argued that, although religion is immutable, religious knowledge is not; it evolves according to time and place. Khatami was offering to spring-clean the Islamic Republic, to change repressive and anachronistic laws.

The next four years were first a time of hope, then of disappointment, and finally of cynicism and despair. Khatami's culture minister unbanned hundreds of banned books and films and music albums. He allowed dozens of newspapers to open. But the conservatives bullied and threatened him and ended up driving him from office. The newspapers were closed down and their owners dragged to court, while the Council of Guardians vetoed every piece of reformist legislation that was passed by parliament.

'Iran cannot be reformed,' Mohsen said. 'Khamenei won't let it happen. The mullahs won't let it happen.' But he and Amin voted for Khatami when they had the chance, in 2001, the president's re-election year. Khatami's second term was a big non-event and the two friends were glad to get shot of him when he stepped down, in 2005. Ahmadinejad was elected after skilfully exploiting a mood of lassitude among many voters and appealing to the conservative instincts of traditional and provincial Iranians. Pretty soon Khatami's tenure started to seem like a golden age.

Mohsen and Amin didn't bother voting in the election that brought Ahmadinejad to power. They turned completely off politics and religion, and even off Soroush – these things only led to disappointment.

After military service Mohsen got a job in a small steel factory east of Tehran. Its owner was a distant relation of Ahmadinejad. He depicted his factory as the acme of modern business practice. In fact it was a sweatshop. The workers had to swipe in at 7.00 in the morning and no one was allowed home before 6 p.m. Some of them lived in Karaj, an hour west of Tehran, so their day began at 4.30 a.m. If they arrived ten minutes late the boss would dock their wages. Mohsen said to his boss, 'If this is the way you treat your workers, they won't feel any loyalty to you or the company and they'll steal from you at the first opportunity.' Mohsen's boss laughed and said, 'First rule of business: know your workers. Don't let them get above themselves . . .'

At the factory the workers cursed the president. 'Son of a whore!' Then one day he came to the factory to open a new unit and it was like the coming of the Hidden Imam, with the workers crying and pressing chits into his hands, and he smiled sleepily and praised the virtue and industry of the Iranian toiler, before getting into his helicopter and flying off again.

One day Mohsen asked permission to take a week's holiday and his boss laughed and said, 'Maybe next year.' That was the last day Mohsen turned up for work at the steel factory.

Mohsen and Amin, who was also unemployed, started talking about going abroad. They would go to Malaysia on student visas and find work. They would go to Istanbul and throw themselves on the mercies of the UN, pretending they were Christian converts, or gay, or both. 'If you send us back to Iran, you'll be condemning us to death!' They would win the lottery for Green Cards and go to America. But Mohsen made excuses for not carrying out these plans. He found that he actually didn't want to leave Iran. He would be lonely and homesick. He dressed up his reluctance as political principle. He told Amin, 'That would be exactly what they want – a nice empty country to run, free of potential troublemakers. A bit like the Shah when he told the opposition, 'Leave, or go to jail!'

At the beginning of May 2009, when Ahmadinejad looked like a shoo-in, Amin said to Mohsen, 'I don't know about you, but if he gets re-elected, I'm out of here. I can't take another four years. So I'm going to vote. Not only am I going to vote; I'm going to campaign for the reformists. That way, if the reformists lose, I'll know that I did my best. I won't carry it around with me for the rest of my life. What do you think? Are you with me?'

Mohsen nodded uneasily. There was another factor. Amin had a new girlfriend, Solmaz. She wore dark lipstick, somewhere between apricot and tobacco. She almost became Mohsen's girlfriend, but then Amin was given a car by his father and she became his. Every now and then Solmaz gave Mohsen a knotted look, a look that seemed to say, 'If you had a car, I would be yours.'

Mohsen thought, 'If Ahmadinejad wins and Amin emigrates, Solmaz will need consoling. I'll emigrate a bit later on, once Amin is settled.'

Mohsen and Amin discussed whom they should support. Apart from Ahmadinejad himself, three candidates had been cleared to run by the Council of Guardians: Mohsen Rezai, Mir-Hossein Mousavi and Mehdi Karrubi. Rezai had been in charge of the Revolutionary Guard during the war. He stood no chance of winning, but he might take a few votes off Ahmadinejad. The real choice, therefore, was between Mousavi and Karrubi.

Mir-Hossein Mousavi was a soft, pale man. He had a flowery nose and thick lenses and a white beard.

Mohsen's father said, 'He's a nonentity.'

Mohsen said, 'But he was prime minister during the war! He steered the country through economic peril!'

His father replied, 'At least he's clean. But he didn't raise a peep when they were busy executing dissidents in jail. Not a peep.'

Since Khomeini's death and the abolition of the post of prime minister, Mousavi had pretty much stayed out of politics; his withdrawal from public life denoted disapproval of the way the country was being run. The reformists had begged Mousavi to run in 2005. He had refused. This time, however, he felt the state of the country was so bad that he had no choice. Inflation and unemployment were high; Ahmadinejad had squandered the country's massive oil revenues on handouts. The Revolutionary Guard had spread its tentacles into all areas of Iranian life: politics, the economy, even sport. Many older Iranians remembered Mousavi with gratitude and affection, for keeping the country on its feet at a time of hardship. And he enjoyed Khatami's support.

Young Iranians knew the cleric Mehdi Karrubi much better. He had been parliamentary speaker when Khatami was president. After standing unsuccessfully for the presidency in 2005, Karrubi had publicly accused Mojtaba Khamenei, the Supreme Leader's son, of committing electoral fraud in Ahmadinejad's favour. Karrubi was blunt, even brave, but there were doubts over his probity.

'Show me a mullah,' Mohsen's father said, 'and I'll show you a thief.'

Solmaz joined the discussion. Solmaz was a women's-rights activist. She was part of the One Million Signatures Campaign, an initiative aimed at gathering signatures for an improvement in women's rights. Some of Solmaz's friends in the movement had met Karrubi, and he had committed himself to radical reforms in favour of women's rights. Mousavi, by contrast, had made much vaguer promises. He had not received the activists in person.

'I agree with Solmaz that in some ways Karrubi is the better candidate,' said Mohsen. 'But a split in the reformist vote can only benefit Ahmadinejad. Mousavi has been endorsed by Khatami and stands a much better chance than Karrubi of beating Ahmadinejad, so we are obliged to support Mousavi.'

In this way, Mohsen, Amin and Solmaz endorsed Mir-Hossein Mousavi for the post of president.

2

Amin will not have to emigrate. Solmaz will never be Mohsen's. The reformists are going to win, cruise it. Tehran has gone ape-shit. The whole city is Mousavi, Mousavi, Mousavi.

June 8, 2009. Mohsen is down at the local Mousavi campaign office. He's wearing a green T-shirt and a green wristband, because, besides being the colour of Islam, green is Mousavi's colour.

Mohsen is speaking to other people decked in green, Faraz and Pegah and Amir-Hossein and a man whom everyone calls the Doctor. The Doctor is a paediatrician and this is his practice. For the past week, he has accepted no patients. He is engaged, he tells people, in trying to cure Iran. If someone comes in seeking medical help for their child, the Doctor refers them to a family clinic up the road. But no one leaves empty-handed. To every poorly child, Faraz gives a poster and a wristband. The children saunter out smiling and happy, raising their arms and giving the V-for-victory sign.

'Ahmadi, bye-bye! Ahmadi, bye-bye!'

The Doctor gets off the phone to a colleague in Kerman. The whole of Kerman is green, he reports, with just one or two neighbourhoods solidly pro-Ahmadinejad. It's a similar story in Khorramabad and Hamadan. 'Ahmadinejad will win in Mashhad and Qom,' says the Doctor, 'and that's it.'

Mohsen takes the Mousavi posters which Pegah has given him and goes into the street outside, down the hill to Vali-ye Asr. It's starting to get dark and the families are coming out of their houses and into the streets. Young people, children chasing each other, leaping over the drainage channels. One child, a gleeful twelve-year-old, his lips Cheetos-pink, points to the monkey on the side of the empty packet.

'One week! Two weeks! Unwashed Mahmoud fairly reeks!'

At the first crossroads the traffic gets heavier. It isn't rush-hour traffic or the beginning of the weekend traffic. It's election traffic. Take a car. Cover the bodywork and side windows with posters, tie green ribbons to the wing-mirrors and aerial, fill up with friends and family. Go and join the party.

Mohsen stands at the crossroads and places rolled-up posters into hands protruding from the open car windows. After a while the cars slow down from the weight of traffic. They are barely moving now, but that doesn't matter; no one is in a hurry to go anywhere. The din increases. Lean on the horn. Some young men have got out of their car and are dancing to Persian hip-hop from the car stereo – gyrating, snapping fingers.

Mohsen sees some of the boys he went to school with: Hatef and Mamali and Hatef's younger brother Sadegh. They are with some girls and they are crouching by the side of the road. They leap into the air and then crouch again. Leap and crouch. It's a version of the childhood game where one person says the name of an object or an animal and the others, if it flies, shout 'fly!' and jump into the air.

'Sparrow!' shouts Mamali.

'Fly!' the others shriek.

'Crow!'

'Fly!'

'Mahmoud!'

'Fly!'

The passers-by stop to watch and laugh. The police are in small groups. They are smiling because the crowd is good-natured and they have orders not to interfere. The past few nights have seen the biggest street crowds in Iran's history, but there has hardly been any violence. Some people in the crowd shout, 'Police! We thank you! Police! We thank you!'

There is a roar from behind Mohsen and he turns and sees a convoy of south-Tehran *soosools*, two to a motorbike, roaring up the pavement. The *soosools* are poor and not very clever and they have come up here, to the centre of Tehran, to show off their green bandannas and their muscles under tight T-shirts. The *soosools* combine machismo with an obsessive, almost effeminate concern for their appearance. They wear tight jeans and do menial jobs and spend their spare time body-building and sculpting their black, shiny hair. Mohsen is contemptuous of *soosools*, but he is pleased to see them here. Their presence shows that Mousavi's supporters extend beyond the urban middle class of conservative caricature. They are a movement.

It's dark now and the traffic has started moving again. Three girls are leaning out of the windows of a car, whooping and flashing the V-sign. God, Iranian girls are beautiful! Mohsen gets into a debate with a Karrubi supporter. Mohsen promises Karrubi a place in Mousavi's cabinet. Whichever portfolio he wants, it's his. The Karrubi man protests vigorously. On the contrary, it's Mousavi who will take pride of place in the Karrubi government; he will have his own super-ministry, limousine and cohort of *houris*. They laugh, exchange posters and kiss each other on the cheek.

Walking up towards Vanak Square, Mohsen bumps into his parents. They stand together at the side of the road and his father buys ice creams. 'Guess who I saw waving a Mousavi flag?' he says with a sly smile, and he names Mohsen's former teacher, a tyrant who once asked Mohsen which members of his family said their prayers. 'Even he,' Mr Abbaspour goes on, 'knows which way the wind is blowing.' Mohsen's mother smiles to herself, a smile that says, 'And we all know other members of the Wind Party.'

Quite suddenly, over the past two weeks, Ahmadinejad has stopped being a dead cert. He has fallen behind Mousavi in the unofficial polls. (There are no official polls.) This is down to people like Mohsen's father. Having insisted for most of the campaign that nothing in the world would induce him to vote, Mohsen's father has changed his mind. He doesn't say as much, but his presence here, in the streets, indicates that he will go to the mosque with the rest of his family on election day and allow himself to be hustled into the polling station, where he will vote for Mousavi. Across the country, people who said they would not vote, or who didn't vote last time, or who have never voted in their lives, have changed their minds.

Mohsen isn't certain why this has happened. Somehow, a feeling has grown that Mousavi might win, and everyone loves a winner. This in turn has encouraged people to abandon their old indifference and cynicism and examine what they really want to happen. They don't want Ahmadinejad to win. They feel strongly that it would be bad for Iran if he did. So they are going to do what Khamenei and the others have been urging them to do. They are going to vote.

Mohsen has crossed Vanak Square now and is progressing further up Vali-ye Asr. Someone shouts, 'It's Mousavi! It's his bus!' The crowd is heaving and craning to try and see up the street, to distinguish the outline of the campaign bus from the field of lights and flashing and noise. Suddenly Solmaz is at his side. She has appeared with two friends and she is laughing, and Mohsen is looking at her white teeth surrounded by dark, apricot-tobacco lips, and at her big determined eyes, and then up at the bus containing Mousavi, inching down the street, and he knows he won't forget this moment.

It's past 11 p.m. on election night. Having spent the day together, touring the polling stations, Mohsen, Amin and Solmaz are going back to their respective families to have dinner and listen to the official results. The end isn't in doubt. Mousavi has already claimed victory. His supporters believe he won at least 60 per cent of the vote. Mohsen, Amin and Solmaz will not sleep tonight. They will go out and celebrate. 'It will be the biggest party in Iran's history,' says Mohsen as they part.

Mohsen lets himself into the apartment. His mother is in the kitchen, cooking his favourite supper of deep-fried cutlets stuffed with minced lamb that has been seasoned and coated with flour. Mohsen will make a sloppy sandwich using cutlets, *taftun* bread, yoghurt, herbs and pickles, and he will wash down his feast with Coke. He intends to eat his triumphal supper in front of the TV, flicking between the various state TV channels, the BBC's new Persian-language channel, which has rolling election coverage, and the Voice of America. The foreign channels are illegal, of course, but almost everyone has a satellite dish in Tehran, because state TV is crap.

Mohsen tells his mother what happened today. He and Amin and Solmaz were among the first to cast their votes at a school near Haft-e Tir Square. They spent the rest of the morning cruising from polling station to polling station in Amin's beat-up Renault 5 – Mohsen and Amin up front, Solmaz in the back. They went as far south as Rey, as far north as Tajrish, and ended up having a late hamburger lunch with some friends in Saadatabad. They used half a tank of gasoline and cried with laughter telling each other Ahmadinejad jokes. They flaunted the ban on election-day campaigning. Solmaz wore a green headscarf belonging to her mother, and green earrings. The boys trailed their arms out of the car windows, flashing V-for-victory signs.

Everywhere they saw foreign journalists and felt pride that the attention of the world was on Iran. Seeing one group of journalists outside a polling station, they leaped out of the car and surrounded them.

'Who do you think will win?' the journalists asked. 'Have you heard the rumours that there will be electoral fraud?' Amin and Mohsen both tried to reply, but their terrible English was an insuperable obstacle, so they started laughing. Solmaz had to answer for all three of them.

As they drove away from the journalists, Mohsen was angry with himself for treating the exchange as a joke. No doubt the foreigners were experienced reporters who had asked the same questions in dozens of other countries at dozens of other elections. But this was

Mohsen's country, Iran, one of the oldest civilisations in the world. There isn't room for jokes when one is discussing Iran!

Mohsen told Amin to stop the car and reverse. When they got back to the journalists, Mohsen turned to Solmaz and said, 'Please translate what I am about to say. This is important. We must show these people that we take the process seriously.' Getting out of the car, he addressed the journalists: 'Dear guests, I have something to add. The scale of the Mousavi vote will make it impossible for electoral fraud to take place. Even if the Council of Guardians decides that Ahmadinejad must win, it will be impossible.' Then, waving his hand over the line of voters, he said, 'These people will not let them.'

Standing over the stove, Mohsen's mother smiles as Mohsen vaunts his patriotism. She tells him to put on his slippers and go and sit down. She will bring his supper through in a few minutes. Mohsen goes into the sitting room. His father is in there, watching the TV, a bowl of sour green plums and figs and tiny wine-coloured grapes on his lap. He eats abstractly, mechanically. Today, at the polling station, he set aside his cynicism and joined a process he doesn't really believe in, and now he feels regret. The Islamic Republic and his family and childish emotion have conspired to make him look a fool.

'Why are you looking so smug?' Mohsen's father is picking a fight.

'Ma!' Mohsen pretends he didn't hear. 'Isn't supper ready yet? I'm starving.'

'The midget is going to win,' his father mutters, but Mohsen ignores him. He knows his father's moods.

'I said the midget is going to walk it.' Louder, this time.

Mohsen turns and stares at his father. 'What?'

Mohsen's father goes on spitefully, 'Haven't you heard? You're part of this benighted election! I'm talking about fraud, fraud on a massive scale. Everything has been prepared; they're leaving nothing to chance. Don't tell me you didn't see Shariatmadari's article! He accused the reformists of already having a strategy ready for disputing their election defeat!'

Mohsen glares at his father. 'What are you saying? You know what's going on out there? Mousavi has already declared victory! He issued a statement to the media. It's as good as over!'

'And why did he issue this statement?' Mr Abbaspour asks sardonically. 'I'll tell you why; to pre-empt the news that people have told him to expect! He knows they're going to stitch him up and he wants to get his version in first.' Mr Abbaspour waves his hand dismissively.

Mohsen has heard the rumours. He read the Shariatmadari article, in the pro-government daily *Kayhan*. He is painfully aware of the fragility of his own optimism. He has lived with this optimism for the past three weeks, and has gotten used to it.

The telephone rings. Mohsen hesitates before picking it up. It's Amin, but his voice, usually calm, has grown panicky and aggressive. 'Have you heard?' he demands. 'The Interior Ministry is saying Ahmadinejad is ahead with sixty-nine per cent of the ballots counted!'

Mohsen turns pale. 'How on earth can they know?' he asks weakly. 'They only just shut the polls!' Suddenly Mohsen can't hear himself think. The BBC is responding to the reports and his father has turned up the volume. Someone is saying that the early results are probably from rural constituencies and small towns – the constituencies that have been declared are all Ahmadinejad strongholds.

'Mohsen shouts into the phone, 'I'll see you down at the campaign office in five minutes! OK?'

Mohsen puts down the phone and immediately it rings. It's his cousin, the one in Italy. He can't believe the news. He was at the Iranian embassy this morning in Rome. Everyone he spoke to was for Mousavi. It was the biggest turnout anyone there could remember. 'The monarchists and the other opposition groups were there, trying to persuade people to boycott the vote, but no one listened. What's going on in Tehran?'

'How should I know?' Mohsen replies abruptly. 'We don't know any more than you do. I'm going to the campaign headquarters now. I'll call you later.' Mohsen phones Faraz from the local

Mousavi campaign. Faraz is better informed than him, but his cellphone is engaged.

Mohsen stumbles into the kitchen where his mother is taking burned cutlets out of the hot oil, patting them with kitchen paper. She mutters, 'Son-of-a-bitch!' Mohsen goes to his room to fetch his wallet and cellphone and then he heads for the door. As he slams it behind him he hears his mother's angry voice from the kitchen: 'It's too early, for God's sake! How could they have counted so quickly?'

The street is dark and empty, but Mohsen can hear the sound of hooting horns from somewhere further west. His instinct has been to assume that any noise of celebration is being made by Mousavi supporters, but this time he must correct himself. The horns are Ahmadinejad horns.

The main road is busy and a crowd has gathered outside the Doctor's surgery. People are standing around outside, talking into cellphones. Pegah is wiping her eyes with a handkerchief. Rumours are flying. Mousavi has been arrested. Mousavi is going to present a formal complaint to the Supreme Leader. Khatami has been to see the Supreme Leader and demanded new elections. Mousavi's house has been surrounded by *Basij* militants and all inside arrested. Mousavi has been threatened with arrest if he sets foot out of his house. Where is he? The house near the presidential palace or his campaign headquarters?

Amin is there. His eyes are shining with sadness and fear. Mohsen says, 'Where do we go to find out the truth?'

Amin points inside the surgery. 'The Doctor is inside trying to speak to the Mousavi people, trying to get more information.'

The surgery is in the same state as it was when the campaign stopped forty-eight hours ago. The trash cans overflow with papers and plastic cups and faxes. One seat has a pile of unused posters. The Doctor is on the phone. The number he is dialling is engaged. He tries, puts the phone down and tries again.

Suddenly someone shouts, 'Quiet! It's Daneshju!' and everyone crowds around a television that someone has put on a table in the corner of the room. Kamran Daneshju, the head of the election commission, is announcing the latest results. He begins by thanking the Iranian people for turning out in exceptionally high numbers, despite the best efforts of the Western media to dissuade people from voting, and then he turns to the votes that have so far been counted. These number 15,251,771, a little under half of the total ballots cast. Then he announces the number of votes that each candidate has garnered so far.

He does this in alphabetical order. The first candidate is Mahmoud Ahmadinejad, who has received 10,230,478 votes. Such is the uproar in the campaign office that only the people near the television hear that Mohsen Rezai has received 259,456 votes and Mehdi Karrubi a risible 132,935. The Doctor raises his hands for silence, but not everyone hears that 4,628,912 votes have been counted for Mir-Hossein Mousavi – just over 30 per cent of the vote.

The people in the campaign headquarters are looking at each other and shaking their heads, and some of them are smiling, too, cynics' smiles. Mohsen feels utter desolation, but he also feels a sharper feeling, the beginning of anger.

He turns to Amin. 'You know what they're saying to us? They're saying to us, "Your votes meant nothing. You came out in record numbers and stood in line and voted, and we will put that in our pockets and consider it to be evidence for your support for the Islamic Republic, but don't make the mistake of thinking we can be bothered to count . . ."'

Mohsen's voice trails off because there has been a sudden commotion at the door. One of the girls screams. Two young Mousavi supporters career towards Mohsen as if they have been pushed very hard. Suddenly the doorway is full of men wearing bottle-green uniforms and four-day stubble. The bottle-green uniforms make way for four men in plain clothes, and from the middle of this small crowd of assailants a leader emerges.

He's a squat, muscular man of about forty-five, bearded and covered in sweat, wearing a white shirt, and his forehead has a perfectly centred disc of calloused skin from excessive prayer. He doesn't introduce himself – doesn't go into his name, rank and affiliation. From his age and appearance, certain things may be inferred.

This man is a member of Iran's military-security complex. He fought in the war with Iraq, has been on the pilgrimage to Mecca a dozen times, considers himself a front-line soldier on behalf of the Hidden Imam, and has hit and tortured people. He inhabits a constellation of atmospheres – impenetrable to most, beautifully logical to anyone on the inside – that consist of the Revolutionary Guard, the *Basij*, the police, the Ministry of Intelligence and the judiciary. The people in these worlds grew up together, fought together and were corrupted together. They are brothers-in-law and buy companies and houses on each other's recommendations. They attend memorial services for each other's parents and help each other's children enter university or get a passport. They worship together and breakfast together during Ramadan. They all enjoy the favour of people close to President Ahmadinejad.

The newcomer is the Islamic Republic in its current, militarised, neo-fascist guise. Before, the mullahs were in charge of every-thing. Now they are being superseded in public affairs by the Revolutionary Guard. The Revolutionary Guard and its protector, Ahmadinejad, regard the clergy as, at best, adornments. The officers don't need their intercession in divine matters because they have a direct line to the Hidden Imam. And he, in turn, is God's ultimate representative on Earth.

The man standing in the doorway of the Doctor's surgery is not a rarity. Every family has someone like him. In recent years, such men have been under control. They have been kept in the shadows by the people, the politicians and the mullahs, who know that it isn't good PR to front a sacred republic with maniacs and criminals. What is happening now, everyone understands, is that this control has been lifted.

The man in the white shirt wears an expression of savage triumph. He surveys the room and the people around him. The Doctor rises from his chair and demands, 'Would you mind telling me . . . ?'

The newcomer interrupts. His voice is quiet but authoritative. 'Who's in charge of this spectacle?'

The doctor walks towards him and says, 'This place is my surgery and . . .'

The man in the white shirt corrects him. 'I want to know who is in charge of political operations here. I'm not interested in what this place is used for when it's not been commandeered by counter-revolutionaries.'

The Doctor draws himself up and says warily, 'Sir, this place was a Mousavi campaign office until the end of official campaigning, two days ago. Since then it has been closed. This evening I put a television in here and opened the doors so that our friends could gather and watch the election results. There are no political operations going on here.'

The man in the white shirt gestures to some Mousavi posters lying around and asks, 'What are these doing here? Have you been campaigning beyond the allotted period?'

The Doctor looks puzzled. 'How would Mr Mousavi benefit,' he asks, 'from our continuing to campaign after the election has taken place?'

The question is impertinent. The man in the white shirt says, 'Sit down' in a voice that is barely audible. Then he orders his men to bring everyone in, even those on the sidewalk outside.

The man in the white shirt is clearly used to speaking in public. He is used to commanding. He is a thinker and a theoriser. He may be the kind of person who attends a huddle in the *Basij* barracks on a Thursday night and gives the *basijis* a blast of political indoctrination after they have beaten their naked chests in time to a votive chant and are glowing and covered in sweat – the kind of guy who makes them feel, thrilled and shivering, like the chosen warriors of Islam.

'I'm going to tell you a story,' he begins. He has a soft Isfahani accent; it contrasts with the hardness of his words. His audience numbers around thirty, crammed into the surgery. 'There was a Japanese soldier,' he goes on, 'and they found him on an island years after the Second World War had ended with Japan's defeat.

This man was still convinced that the war was going on. He was quite mad and it took a long time before they convinced him that Japan had lost the war, and that it was in his best interests to come to terms with the catastrophe that had taken place.'

The man in the white shirt has stopped sweating. He strides around the room, looking at his audience. He casts a contemptuous eye over the women there, young women for the most part with inadequate *hejab*. 'I don't know what happened to the Japanese soldier, whether he was reintegrated into society, or whether he died, broken and abandoned, but the choice that faced him is the choice now facing you.' The man in the white shirt allows himself a fleeting smile of contempt. 'For this,' he goes on, 'is what you resemble, here in your squalid little campaign centre with your filthy flyers and wristbands' – he glances at the chair, which is overflowing with posters.

'You choose the colour green,' he goes on, 'the colour of Islam, and you chant the slogans of the revolution and call on the memory of the late Imam Khomeini, like the Hypocrites that you are. You may have fooled a few gullible children in north Tehran, a few rich kids, but you haven't fooled the majority of Iranians, for they have learned the lesson of the unfortunate, virtuous Imam Ali, which is to beware the enemy offering false reassurance.' The man in the white shirt withdraws a small metal object from his pocket. It is a pair of pliers. With it, he picks up one of the Mousavi campaign posters sitting on the chair in front of him and drops it to the floor. He sits down.

'A mere two days have elapsed since the end of the campaign, since the end of our war, but the effect of these two days is the same as the effect of all those years on the Japanese soldier. You and he are the same. You are obsolescent because you persist, even now, in dreaming your dreams of anarchy and overthrow, under the cover of a legitimate election campaign.' His voice is now harsh and loud. 'The president received the endorsement of more than two-thirds of the electorate, and the closest of his challengers barely thirty per cent of the vote. Is it possible for anyone to contest his victory? No! The war is over, but there will always be a handful who fight on, crazed and embittered, and it is my responsibility – the responsibility of anyone who cares for Iran's future – to make sure that they cannot damage the country.'

He orders one of his men to take photographs of everyone in the room. The cop has a small digital camera. 'Don't forget to smile,' says the man in the white shirt; 'we don't want your friends in the human-rights organisations to get the impression you've been ill treated.' The two policemen are emerging from the toilet; they have damp faces and are doing up their cuffs. 'Your prayers will have to wait,' he says curtly; 'I want you to arrest this so-called doctor, this man who turns away patients in order to campaign for the favoured candidate of counter-revolutionaries, and put him in my car.'

'You're going to take him away? What for? What crime has he committed? Where is your warrant?'

It's a young voice, indignant and without fear, and when everyone turns round and looks at Mohsen, he realises that it's his.

The man in the white shirt also turns to Mohsen. He seems pleased. He nods in recognition. Mohsen wears a worn pair of jeans and a blue short-sleeved shirt and white sneakers. He has gelled his hair and his cheeks are smooth. He is a young Iranian man who likes photography, modern Persian poetry and the banned Iranian pop group Atlas. Mohsen is destroying the revolution with his indifference to the ideals that animate it, and his conviction that much of what he learned at school is a burdensome irrelevance. Mohsen is quietly, good-naturedly fighting to impose his taste and aesthetic on the taste and aesthetic of God.

Standing there, reddening, Mohsen has a choice. He can either return the official's stare or bow his head and hope for leniency. To look down is not only to make a tactical retreat. It is to accept implicitly the statements of the man in the white shirt. To look back insolently is to argue that no offence has been committed, that there is nothing to be ashamed of. It's easy enough to think such thoughts here, in the warmth of the Doctor's surgery; the test will come outside the surgery, in the darker, dirtier environs of a compound, complex or station. Mohsen is unable to lower his head. He returns the man's stare.

There is silence in the campaign office. Suddenly someone's cellphone rings. The ring tone is Abjeez' 'I Could Have', a banned pop song. A girl scrabbles in her bag, frantically trying to withdraw her cellphone from among her other possessions and turn it off. 'Give me the handset,' says the man in the white shirt. He takes the phone, making ostentatiously sure that his hand does not touch hers, and drops it into his pocket. 'You can pick this up in a few days,' he says lightly; he and the girl both know she won't see it again.

The man in the white shirt turns back to Mohsen and says, 'I know who you are. I know who you are better than you do yourself. There are lots of you around the place, wasting space, but thankfully not as many as there are of us. I should take you in as well, but I've only been authorised to arrest the head of the campaign office, and I never exceed my orders because that would be the beginning of anarchy.'

The Doctor is being hustled out of the room. His face is drained, he has been condemned already. The man in the white shirt turns for a last look into the campaign office. 'I'll tell you all something interesting,' he announces. 'If I were a filthy apostate like you lot, I'd make a bet right now. I'd put down big money. You know what I'd bet?' The man in the white shirt points at Mohsen, remembering his face. 'I'd bet that this young man won't survive the summer.'

After he has gone and the girls are crying, Amin sidles up and hisses, 'Mohsen! I thought you were a goner! Don't you know when to keep your mouth shut?' But Mohsen has slumped into a chair in front of the television, wondering if he will ever have the energy to get up, wondering what is going to happen next.

On the TV some analysts are congratulating officials from the Council of Guardians and the Interior Ministry on their industry and speed. 'It's a remarkable achievement,' says one analyst, 'to have counted thirty-five per cent of the votes a mere three hours after the polling stations closed.' Another man enthuses, 'It's more than that. It's a testament to the selflessness and hard work of the officials involved, and a stinging slap for the foreign enemies of Islam and Iran. Our beloved viewers will no doubt recall America's so-called election of 2000, in which George Bush was declared to have defeated his opponent, Gore, despite polling fewer votes than him, and where the Supreme Court overruled the express wishes of the American people! And the Americans have the nerve to lecture the rest of the world about holding free and fair elections!'

The analyst stops talking and the presenter looks serious. 'Let us remind our dear viewers that there is no way of knowing how this election will end, for although one of the candidates is leading, a huge number of votes remain to be counted. This, however, can be said with cast-iron certainty: our glorious election has already displayed to the world the qualities of Iranian democracy!'

Two conflicts, separate but related, are taking shape tonight, with the consequence that events in Iran begin to move with exceptional speed. Iranians are not used to things moving quickly. Stability is the watchword; that means the leaden hand of autocracy and the nerve ends of the people numbed from the weight. Now there is a new dispensation; the hand is lifted, the blood starts to rush. Over one week, from June 13 to June 19, Iranians run and shout. The country will not be the same again.

The first conflict involves the people at the top. Revolutions eat themselves. Why does the cannibalistic instinct run strong in people who pledged, in their youth, loyalty and brotherhood? After the election results a group of once-solid revolutionaries are invited, by the Supreme Leader, senior commanders of the Revolutionary Guard and state TV, to step into line. Let us unite in celebrating the electoral turnout, they are urged, higher by ten million votes than any electoral turnout to date. Let us not quibble over the details – a stuffed ballot box here, a little voter intimidation there. And for those who refuse this invitation, there is a warning. If you do rock the boat, your fate will be that of Bani-Sadr, a former disciple of Khomeini who was anathema-tised after he split from the hardliners; or of Rajai, whose group-uscule, the Hypocrites, lost an armed conflict with the regime in the early 1980s, and survives, a vulgar personality cult, on Western charity. Or, looking further back, it will be the fate of those early rebels who dared to rise up against the Prophet of God.

Never have the reformists been threatened so overtly, so un-ambiguously. Until recently, internal enemies went tactfully unnamed; they were referred to as 'certain circles', or 'those who have been gulled by the West', or 'a handful of malcontents'. Now, for the first time, the schisms have been acknowledged and the reformists are publicly accused of being counter-revolutionaries. There is Mr Mousavi, who happens to be a former prime minister and former confidant of the Imam. There is Mr Karrubi, a mullah, who was appointed by the Imam to run a big charitable organ-isation, and who went on to be parliament speaker. There is Mr Khatami, also a mullah, who was President of the Islamic Republic for eight years. Finally, and perhaps most important, there is Mr Rafsanjani, yet another mullah, a second former president – the Islamic Republic's perennial Number Two. Towards the end of his life, the Imam was closer to Rafsanjani than to anyone else. A cold man, cunning, brave, as rich as Croesus. In the second half of the Iran–Iraq War, Rafsanjani hurled hundreds of thou-sands of Iranians to their deaths in suicidal offensives; later, as president, he allowed agents from the Intelligence Ministry to murder dozens of intellectuals and writers. But he is old now, and he wants history to remember him as a good guy. His old friend Ayatollah Khamenei also feels the hand of mortality, but history will probably be less kind to him. The two men have fallen out because of the past, and because Khamenei is supportive of Rafsanjani's sworn enemy, President Ahmadinejad.

There is something to be gained, from the hardliners' point of view, from naming an internal foe. An atmosphere of hostility and intimidation builds – he may be cowed into silence or inaction. But there is a risk, also, for no one is blind to the fact that today's counter-revolutionaries were yesterday's leading revolutionaries and pillars of the establishment. What has happened to the revolution, the people ask, that yesterday's office-holders should now be today's traitors and toadies? Certainty turns to uncertainty. The people who today describe each other using choice insults – liar, thief – were once great friends and colleagues. What does it tell us about the ship of state if the captain and officers are wrestling for the wheel?

The people are inclined to forgive the reformists for changing, for the people have changed as well. Do we have a record of Mr Mousavi, as prime minister, raising his voice against the executions, the policies of intimidation, the cultural slash-and-burn? We do not. What about Khatami, Karrubi and Rafsanjani? Not a peep. Those who are today being accused of counter-revolutionary plotting accused their enemies of the same crimes only a decade or two ago. These enlightened people, who question the competence of one, fallible man, the Supreme Leader, to embody the will of God and distil His wishes – these are the very men who regarded Khomeini's word as law, and deviation from Khomeini's word as deviation from the will of God. There is an awkward discrepancy between what these people used to believe and what they believe now.

What are we witnessing here: a fight between different parts of the same sclerotic system? What's at stake? The future form of the revolution, or its very survival? The answers to these questions change over a remarkably short period, between June 12 and June 19. When they go to the polling stations, the supporters of Mousavi and Karrubi do so as adherents to the Islamic Republic – they see change as a distant but achievable prospect, and this emboldens them to vote. After the announcement of the first official results, however, things start to change. People aren't objecting to the fact that they lost, but to the fact that their votes don't seem to have been counted. The Iranians are a proud people. It takes a lot for them to get angry; suddenly, when it's least expected, they get really mad.

How sure can we be that the election was stolen? Isn't it

the case, as the government's supporters point out, that Ahmadinejad's supporters live outside the city centres, in the poor suburbs and provincial towns and villages – that they constitute the country's 'silent' majority? Well, yes and no. There is something distasteful about Ahmadinejad's attempt to paint himself as the anti-establishment underdog, because he enjoys the support of Iran's vast military and paramilitary apparatus. Furthermore, Iran is now largely an urban society. A huge number of Iranian town-dwellers are middle-class, relatively well-educated and reluctant to accept at face value the old revolutionary tropes.

In an election that wasn't monitored by outside observers, and where the organisers and observers are all closely associated with the government, you'd be lucky to find a smoking gun. But how to vouch for the cleanliness of the electoral process if the majority of ballot boxes were not verified and confirmed to be empty before voting began, if the majority of the candidates' delegates, empowered by law to observe the process at every polling station, were in fact prevented from doing so, if the number of ballots cast in some constituencies exceeded the number of eligible voters? What conclusions should be drawn if the election is being organised and monitored by two institutions, the Interior Ministry and the Council of Guardians, whose members are avowedly pro-Ahmadinejad, and when the country's only legal broadcasting company acts as the president's mouthpiece? Later, when the results are announced and then confirmed, there is a remarkable uniformity of voting patterns across the country, with the incumbent's share of the vote barely fluctuating from the beginning of the counting process to the end – not to mention his surprising triumphs in Kurdistan, where he is roundly loathed, and in the home provinces, respectively, of Mousavi and Karrubi. Even the fourth presidential candidate, Mohsen Rezai, no friend of the reformists, swiftly asserts that there is something very suspicious about this election.

In cases such as this, when the system cannot move, when the different organs are pushing against each other and the result is paralysis, eyes turn to the ultimate authority. This is the Supreme Leader, Ayatollah Khamenei, and although we know in our hearts that he is a power-hungry conservative, a supporter of the very institutions the reformists accuse of cheating and lying, we pray for him to adopt the position of impartiality that behoves his office. Some remember the youthful Khamenei, black-bearded and cultured, a friend to modernist poets, a music-lover. This is the approachable Khamenei, but we never see him. We see the distant Khamenei, supreme only in name, captive to his constituency, jealous and susceptible to flattery.

It is possible, even probable, that this schism would not have opened up were it not for a parallel and interconnected schism between the rulers and the ruled. It's to hide this schism, and to deny its existence, that the regime urges the voters to come out and vote – it's what prevents the Council of Guardians from vetoing everyone except their favoured candidate. But this second schism would not have emerged with the force that it has, without the first. For it was Mousavi and Karrubi, those former revolutionaries, who refused to accept the election results when they were announced, Mousavi who raised the spectre of a 'governance of lies and dictatorship'.

In the hours following the election, as the streets of the capital fill with angry Iranians, as the accusations and counter-accusations start to fly, you find millions of Iranians praying that Khamenei will draw the country back from the brink, that he will do the right thing.

It's 11 a.m. on June 14. Mohsen is passing near Vali-ye Asr Square. He is on his way home from visiting his grandmother, who is recovering from a bypass operation in a hospital nearby, when he sees a huge crowd. 'What's going on?' he asks a passer-by. 'Victory rally,' comes the reply. Mohsen sees Iranian flags above a mass of Ahmadinejad supporters.

Having spent the past month swimming in exuberant reformist crowds, he wonders what an Ahmadinejad crowd would be like. He pulls out his shirt so that the tails flap, unrolls his sleeves and buttons up his cuffs. He looks in a shop window. He hasn't shaved for a couple of days, and his cheeks are stubbly. Could he pass for an Ahmadinejad supporter? He does up his top button for good measure.

When Mohsen is close enough to see the gritty faces and pitiless eyes, he almost regrets trying to know his enemy any better. Composing himself, he decides to buy a newspaper from a nearby stall. Being surrounded by Ahmadinejad supporters, he chooses *Kayhan*. Flicking through *Kayhan* as he walks, he learns that the Western powers are fuming at the 'heavy blow' they have been dealt by the Iranian electorate. The editorialist sees a comparison between reformist protesters burning dumpsters and Don Quixote tilting at windmills.

Mohsen is at the edge of the crowd. It is segregated according to sex, and he is standing near the women's section. A large group of women wearing chadors hold red flags that someone must have given them, and that carry Qur'anic inscriptions. These women glare and shout shrilly. He hears one say, 'These people are lizards! They say they want to save the republic, but in fact they want to take us back to the time of Zavala Kataf, when the king died and they placed the crown over the belly of his pregnant wife and said, "Long live the King!"'

It's meant to be a victory parade, but the faces around him are taut and angry. Moving into the male section, his gaze rests on a *basiji* who reminds him for a moment of the man in the white shirt who took away the Doctor. In fact there is hardly any physical similarity between the two – rather their expression, of mirthless vindication, is the same. Up on the dais, someone is singing a homily to the virtues of Fatemeh Zahra, the Prophet's daughter and wife of the Imam Ali, whose birthday it is.

Mohsen is relieved to see some young men speaking in low voices and laughing nearby. He instinctively moves closer to them. One of them, a short, thickset young man, is telling the others about the previous night in Tehranpars, where he lives. 'We found two *soosools* spray-painting the wall,' he says. 'They were writing, "Give us back our vote!" Of course, we intervened.'

The thickset man and his friends interrogated the terrified young boys in the shadows, pushing them and asking about their political and religious beliefs. 'You reformists are all sodomites, aren't you?' one of them said.

The thickset young man's voice drops. 'We got one of them to undo his pants and pretend to be fucking the other.' His friends giggle. 'We wanted to see if he got a hard-on!'

'And did he?' Everyone laughs.

'No, but he almost shit himself, he was so terrified! We got them to write, "Our vote, Ahmadinejad," and "Mousavi is a traitor", and let them go.'

The conversation turns to more general subjects. 'These rioters who go out every night,' one of the young men says, 'think they enjoy public support, but the Iranian people will never support rioters who burn and destroy public property and prevent decent people from living their daily lives.' Suddenly he looks towards Mohsen. 'Don't you agree, my friend?'

Mohsen returns the man's stare. He looks for malicious intent, but finds none in his flat, believing expression. It hasn't occurred to these boys that a Mousavi supporter might infiltrate their meeting. Mohsen answers, 'You know what the rioters remind me of? In the Second World War there was a Japanese soldier and they found him years after the war had finished, starved and half-mad, on some island in the Pacific Ocean. They had to break the news to him that the war had been lost and the emperor had surrendered. He was brought back to Tokyo and they put him in a nursing home. He was a tourist attraction; people used to come and see him rave. This is what the reformists remind me of. They fight on without realising the war has been lost. They have become a museum attraction.'

The others nod sagely. 'A good comparison,' says the thickset man.

'Idiot!' Mohsen thinks to himself.

Suddenly the crowd gives a huge cheer. Ahmadinejad has appeared on the dais. He holds his hands above his head. He grins. He places his hand over his chest and bows. There is more cheering. People are shouting the name of their president. He raises his hand for quiet.

Then, as Ahmadinejad starts to speak, Mohsen finds that he feels sick. What possessed him to come here, to hear this man describe the virtues of Fatemeh Zahra as if they are his own, to witness his lying and insincerity and hear him grovel in front of people for whom he feels nothing but contempt?

Mohsen starts moving back through the crowd to the boundary of the square. The people frown as he elbows his way past. They can't understand why, with Ahmadinejad in full flow, someone has decided to leave. At length Mohsen reaches the edge of the square. Behind the crowd a troop of uniformed *basijis* sit on a low wall with some paving stones behind it, swinging their legs. Some of them fondle their truncheons. Others have laid them on the wall. They are watching, rapt.

Mohsen swings himself over the wall. He's a few paces from the sidewalk that leads into Vali-ye Asr Street. But his attention has been caught by something that has fallen onto the paving stones behind the wall. It's a truncheon. It must belong to one of the *basijis* who were sitting on the wall, their backs to him. It must have fallen off the wall and onto the paving stones without its owner noticing.

Mohsen drops to his knees next to the truncheon and pretends to be doing up his shoelace. He quickly unzips his bag, puts the truncheon inside and goes to find a bus to take him to the meeting at Amin's house.

It was Mohsen's idea to hold the meeting in Amin's parents' house. Amin isn't enthusiastic, but this house has a back yard surrounded by high walls. It's possible to sit in this back yard and have a discussion without fearing that you're being overheard.

Amin's family members are unlikely to disturb the meeting. Amin's father is in Shiraz. A relation has died and there is mourning and paperwork. Amin's pregnant sister Shayda, who has moved back home now that her husband has started military service, is keeping an appointment for a scan at the hospital.

Fearing disturbances in the streets, it occurred to her to put off the appointment, but the signs are that the protests are going to get worse, not better, increasing the likelihood of a hiatus in hospital services. 'You never know,' Shayda's mother told her this morning, 'today might be your last chance. We'll go to the hospital together and then you just sit at home and take care of yourself and the little one.'

'If it's a boy,' says Shayda, only half-joking, 'I'm going to call him Mir-Hossein!'

Shayda and her mother left for the hospital at 4.30 p.m. and no one expects them back until well after dark. 'Even if they manage to finish the scan by seven,' Mohsen says, 'it'll take them a couple of hours to come home.' The previous evening, several Tehran neighbourhoods were walled in by noise and cars, the drivers leaning on their horns, and the main roads were littered with burning dumpsters. This evening most people expect a repeat.

Waiting for everyone to turn up, standing with Mohsen and Solmaz, Amin is nervous. He stands at the open door, fingering his goatee and squinting down the street for any sign of *basijis* or informers.

There is a small *Basij* barracks in the next street. Yesterday evening the barracks became an organ of propaganda. 'Death to the Hypocrites!' the *basijis* shouted from their prayer room inside, their voices electronically amplified. 'Death to Israel!' Then the *basijis* went out and set up a roadblock, stopping passing cars and checking them for incriminating objects – green bandannas, Mousavi posters, banned CDs. They swaggered like an invading army, scrawny boys from beyond the southern suburbs, with half-moustaches and chins full of pimples. Only as *basijis* do they feel wanted and complete.

While they wait, Mohsen tells his friends about his truncheon. 'I have it here,' he says, unzipping his bag. He brings out the truncheon. It is black and rubbery. It hits his palm with a smack.

Solmaz is furious. 'Why did you take it?'

'It's my trophy,' Mohsen replies uneasily, 'They'll skin that *basiji* alive when they realise he lost his truncheon.'

'Yes, but that's not the whole story, is it?' says Solmaz. 'You could have got rid of it. But you decided to keep it. Why?' Solmaz is looking at him intently.

'OK,' Mohsen shrugs. 'It's a weapon. I would use it. If they use violence, we should use it back. Why should they use violence and not us?'

Solmaz shakes her head. 'Do you realise what you're saying?'

Until now, politics has been about using an asymmetrical arsenal: civil society, superior arguments, non-violent displays of defiance. It's Solmaz who best understands this, through her involvement with the One Million Signatures Campaign. But now the rules of engagement are changing.

She turns on Mohsen angrily. 'If we use violence, we'll lose.'

Mohsen drops the truncheon back into the bag and does up the zip. Hatef and Mamad are at the door and he doesn't want them to see it.

At about 3 a.m. last night, Mamad tells the others, an armoured truck drove up and stood outside the *Basij* barracks for half an hour, its motor running. According to Mamad, the barracks was emptied of a quantity of arms – this would suggest that the *basijis* fear the barracks will be overrun. Hatef has heard a different rumour, to the effect that the vehicle wasn't taking away arms, but bringing them in. If this is true, it means the *basijis* are preparing to shoot people.

It's a national crisis and hundreds of thousands of *basijis* have been placed on alert around the country. Mohsen has heard that each *basiji* is to receive $50 for every day he is on standby. 'I'll join up immediately,' Solmaz jokes. She has vowed to boycott the university entrance exams that she is due to take in a few weeks. 'I won't sit an exam while Ahmadinejad is president! Then we go on and launch a national strike!'

Gradually, more and more people arrive for the meeting. Amin checks that every new arrival has left his or her cellphone at home. It's common knowledge that Nokia-Siemens, Iran's main cellphone network provider, supplied the authorities with software that enables them to eavesdrop on cellphone conversations. Some also fear that the authorities can listen in on live conversations being conducted in the vicinity of the phone, making the handset a bugging device even when it's turned off.

The young people attending the meeting are sad and proud and scared. To everyone's surprise, even their own, Iranians have not dropped their shoulders and swallowed the insult. Mousavi and Karrubi have done what no reformist leader has ever done, and what the hardliners, when they stole this election, never expected them to do. The hardliners based their predictions on the behaviour of former President Khatami, who spent eight years in power shying from a confrontation, refusing the hardliners' offer of a dirty, one-sided fight. But Mousavi and Karrubi have demanded that the authorities annul the elections and allow the people to come out and demonstrate.

For the moment Mousavi and Karrubi are free, and they have an Internet connection.

It's the first time in the adult lives of these young people that Iran is the centre of the world. Iran is on the front page of every newspaper. It's the lead item of every bulletin. This isn't because the president has said the Holocaust didn't happen, or because he wants to nuke Israel, but because the Iranian people are thrilling the world with their anger and their will to resist.

It's not only Obama and Sarkozy and Brown and Merkel who are glued to their TV sets, brushing up their Iranian history, composing responses. The Iranian community abroad has mobilised itself, launching demonstrations outside embassies and consulates belonging to the Islamic Republic of Iran. In the past, young Iranians like Mohsen felt estranged from these expatriates – rich, well-scrubbed young Americans and Europeans who haven't seen the country in thirty years, or, in the case of the younger generation, at all. Their priorities often seemed to vary from those of Iranians living inside the country. The expats dreamed of upheaval, revolution and other fantasies, but they were too scared to set foot back in Iran. Now, for the first time, everyone seems to be in agreement. An election has been stolen. It should be given back.

The meeting is attended by around fifteen people. About half of them are young men roughly of Mohsen's age. Some of them are university students. Others are trying to get into university. Others have graduated and are looking for work. There are some young women; two of them are from the Karrubi campaign, and get teased. There is a divorcee called Shadi, a primary-school teacher in her mid-forties, who wasn't part of the campaign, but now feels morally obliged to get involved. And there is an old man, Mr Ghorbani, who has come along, Amin whispers, because he is bored at home and wants some tea.

One or two people are scared that the man in the white shirt will reappear, but Amin has put his thirteen-year-old brother Bijan on the door, and Bijan is confident that no one is watching the entrance to the house. Everyone sits in the back yard, underneath the quince tree, talking about what has been going on. Communication among the activists is starting to get harder. The mobile-phone network came down at around lunchtime. It's impossible to send texts.

'They arrested Mirdamadi and Tajzadeh!' someone says. They are leading reformists. Under Khatami they were members of the establishment. Now they are criminals.

'And Ramazanzadeh!' says another. Ramazanzadeh was the government spokesman for a time. Before that, he was governor of Kurdistan.

They are picking off the reformists, one by one. What do they intend to do with them? Everything has been planned in advance. A prosecutor is rumoured to have signed the arrest warrants even before the elections took place!

'Did you hear what Ahmadinejad said today?' says Mamad. 'In his press conference he compared the protesters to football supporters who were angry because their team had lost.' Shadi frowns. 'I thought he called the protesters "chaff".' There is an animated conversation about what Ahmadinejad said, and a consensus is eventually reached. It seems that Ahmadinejad has, at different times on the same day, delivered two gross insults to his compatriots.

'Malodorous swine!' Pegah spits out, and everyone starts laughing.

Before she got married, Pegah was a section head at one of the national newspapers. She knows how to chair a meeting. She holds up her hand and says, 'I think we should try and address things in a logical order. First, I think everyone wants to know what news we have of the Doctor.'

Hatef, Mohsen's old school friend, is the Doctor's nephew. During the campaign Hatef was proud of his association with the Doctor. Now he is pale and afraid. Over the past day and a half, he tells the others, members of the family have been working to get news. Hatef and the Doctor's wife started at the nearest police station, where they were treated with derision. They went on to the neighbourhood *Basij* barracks, one street over from the Abbaspours' house, where they almost got arrested. This morning Hatef and his father, the Doctor's elder brother, went to a branch of the Interior Ministry that deals with people who have disappeared. After standing in line for hours, they were given missing-person forms to fill in. The Doctor's wife stood all morning with her mother outside Evin Prison, with scores of other people, but the official who had reportedly promised to see them failed to appear.

'Who is this man who you say took him away?' they were asked on several occasions. 'What is his name? Give us a physical description.'

A short, muscular Isfahani in a white shirt.

'You may as well go home,' was the advice of a sympathetic conscript standing guard outside Evin. 'You'll be contacted when they want you to know.'

Rumours have begun to fly. The detainees haven't been taken to Evin, but to Revolutionary Guard safe-houses outside the jurisdiction of the Intelligence Ministry and the judiciary. In the old days, the Intelligence Ministry was the most feared weapon in Iran's arsenal of repression. Nowadays that distinction belongs to the Revolutionary Guard; by comparison, the ministry is considered soft. Over the past three days, it is rumoured, scores or even hundreds of people have exited the criminal-justice system and landed in a parallel system, set up by the Revolutionary Guard, leaving no trace.

'What can we do?' The Doctor's young wife wept, bent double, outside Evin Prison.

'Pray,' said the conscript.

This morning brought a clue – or a false lead. The Doctor's wife was passing in front of the neighbourhood *Basij* barracks. As she passed, she looked up, wondering if her husband was inside. A *basiji* stood guard at the door. She had not seen this *basiji* before. As she walked, he hissed, 'Salehi arrested him!'

The Doctor's wife stopped in her tracks, whirled towards the *basiji* and implored him, 'Please tell me more. Tell me where he's being kept! Please!' At that moment a couple of other men walked out of the barracks. The *basiji* abruptly changed his tone. 'How should I know?' he demanded. 'Go to the judicial authorities like anyone else! Go on, be off!'

Anger is on the faces of many of the people sitting under the quince tree. They can no longer bear to be trampled and destroyed. They are the sort of young people who might do something reckless.

Pegah was an older sister to many of them in their youth, as they ranged across this rectangle of central Tehran streets, getting into trouble. Pegah alludes to Mousavi's and Karrubi's orders that all protests must be peaceful and non-confrontational. 'Violence is a trap that is being set for us,' says Pegah. 'We mustn't fall in.' Solmaz glares at Mohsen.

Pegah is the best connected of everyone here. She has friends who worked in Mousavi's main HQ, and of course she knows all the journalists. This morning she was at Karrubi's newspaper, and she brings exciting news, that either tomorrow or the next day there is to be a massive demonstration demanding the annulment of the election. Mousavi and Karrubi will attend.

'They'll never get a permit,' says someone.

'They'll hold the demo whether they have a permit or not.'

Mohsen exclaims, 'This is the new Iran, the Iran they wanted. No longer do we sit around waiting for them to toss us crumbs. We rally, whatever they say.'

'If that doesn't work,' someone else says, 'we go for a general strike!'

How many times, during the Khatami presidency, did the people indicate their willingness to follow their leaders into the streets? How many times were the people disappointed by their leaders' reluctance to risk their own or anyone else's skin? The use of mass action is no longer a monopoly in the hands of the hardliners. This change has happened in the past thirty-six hours.

Not everyone thinks like Pegah. Last night, a few hours after Khamenei confirmed the election results, Mamad and some of his friends went out to set fire to dumpsters in Abbasabad. As he recounts his experiences, Mamad doesn't acknowledge that he was more than an eyewitness, but it's clear from his proud expression that he participated with gusto.

'They pulled the driver of a bus out of his cab. They set fire to the bus and the whole neighbourhood came out to watch it burn.' Mamad's smile is the smile of someone who, after two decades of anonymity, is making his mark.

The *basijis* arrived at a trot to take their revenge. An innocent bystander, a man carrying groceries who had taken refuge in a doorway and was making a rush for home, got a smashed ankle – his screams could be heard in the surrounding side-streets. The *basijis* broke into three residential blocks either side of Abbasabad, allegedly searching for incendiary substances, and turned several apartments upside down. 'It shows how nervous they are,' Mamad says proudly.

Solmaz is infuriated. 'Do you want to reduce us to their level?' she demands with venom. Do you regard the people burning buses on Abbasabad as real Mousavi or Karrubi supporters? I can tell you, I don't! They're no better than *agents provocateurs*! Didn't you see the TV news last night? They showed your burning buses again and again. Why do you think that is? They can convince people that this is the future of Iran, if we win and Mousavi becomes president. They want to tell people that if the election result is overturned, Iran will become another Iraq, another Afghanistan.'

Shadi, the woman in her mid-forties, takes Solmaz's side. 'She's right. We're standing at the beginning of a movement, something we can't see the end of, and attacking police stations and *basijis* is the best way of making sure it's extinguished. This isn't like '78, you know – we haven't been trained to kill and we don't know how to withstand torture. What we have is something much more precious. We have a civil society, we know the value of non-violent resistance. And you all seem to be forgetting that we are a part of a much wider network of world politics and public opinion. We need public opinion abroad to be on our side. If we enjoy foreign support right now, that's partly because people abroad associate this movement with non-violence. If that stops being the case, people around the world will stop supporting us and it will be much easier for the system to stamp the movement out.'

Mohsen is listening too. He is attracted by Shadi's quiet assurance, and slightly awed by her experience, but he finds himself thinking contrary things. He thinks, 'Hold on! Didn't we have a revolution, exactly thirty years ago? Wasn't it your revolution – you and people like you? The failure of your revolution is the reason we now have to go into the streets and set fire to buses! If there had been no revolution, the Shah would have died of cancer and his young son would have become Shah and the country would have been reformed in stages. And by now we'd have something like the constitutional government that Iranian democrats have been promising us since the beginning of the nineteenth century. And here you sit, telling us about our agitation, telling us how to go about things?'

Dusk has fallen. Some of the friends drift away. Others arrive. Pegah looks at her watch and says, 'Everyone onto the roof!'

Amin shows the way. It's a pleasant evening, not too warm.

There is a breeze. They stand up there, peering through the darkness towards the other roofs, chatting self-consciously. They stay several minutes and then someone says, 'It looks as though it won't happen tonight.'

Someone else says, 'You never can tell with these rumours.'

Mohsen says, 'Well, someone has to be first. Why not us?' This prompts an animated discussion, which Pegah interrupts. 'Shush! Listen!' Silence descends on the party and from somewhere behind, probably an apartment block on the next alley, they hear the sound of several male voices.

'*Allahu Akbar!*'

A second later, a group of predominantly female voices respond from a different roof.

'*Allahu Akbar!*'

And so it starts, from different roofs, all around. Two or three people here, more over there. Some people have thrown open their windows and shout from the sill. Many more are on the roofs of their apartment blocks – Mohsen makes out the shapes of the people on nearby roofs, a glint from a pair of spectacles, a cigarette-glow. The neighbourhood is bounded by main roads, but as the chorus grows in volume and intensity, the growl of traffic becomes irrelevant.

There are twenty-odd people up here, and they outshout every roof in the vicinity. Everyone is smiling – even Hatef. Into this old revolutionary slogan, so chilling to the monarch, they pour their sadness and anger. Everyone realises that in 2009 *Allahu Akbar* means something different from *Allahu Akbar* in 1979. No longer is it a call for religion. It has become a call for truth. And it is a mischievous call, for it dares the authorities to declare *Allahu Akbar* a counter-revolutionary slogan! Whoever dreamed up this revival, Mohsen thinks, is a genius.

As he shouts, Mohsen goes to the edge of the roof to look into the street. Shadi quickly advises him to get back. It's a hangover from the revolution. Back then, she explains, it wasn't unknown for police marksmen to pick off people who shouted *Allahu Akbar* from the streets below.

After a while, the shout changes.

'Mir-Hossein!' shouts one roof.

'Ya Hossein!' responds another.

Later, when the night becomes silent again and the party goes downstairs, Mohsen falls in step with Shadi. She smiles wistfully. 'That was a strange memory from the revolution.'

Mohsen grins. 'Do you think we're going to have another one?'

3

June 15: the best day of his life. The best day in the best week of his life. Now, for the first time, not being forced to take orders, not having to listen to idiots, not being patronised, not being humiliated. Not having Ahmadinejad or Khamenei speak for him. No more hearing that the Iranian people want so-and-so or the Iranian people feel such-and-such. For the first time, speaking without a hand weighing on his shoulder or something sticking in his back.

The government is scared. The whole regime is scared. The helicopters circling overhead, state TV, the *basijis* skulking in their barracks; all scared. In years to come, when the edifice comes down and the archives and telephone intercepts are made public, when the principals write their memoirs and chauffeurs spill the beans, we will know what happened out of view – just as we know how the Shah and his ministers and generals dithered and procrastinated, first during the disturbances of 1963 and then in the late 1970s, with the advocates of pitiless repression rounding on the appeasers and both represented in the monarch. We'll learn about crucial meetings between Khamenei and Ahmadinejad and the men around them, about messages between the head of the Revolutionary Guard, the intelligence minister and the chief of police. We'll hear about other men, men whose names we don't yet know, who exert anonymous control over people's lives. There will be ribaldry mixed in with the horror: *Mein Kampf* meets *Catch 22*.

For now, our view is from the ground.

Last night there was another meeting. Everyone wanted to talk about the attack that the security forces launched early that morning on protesting students in a dormitory block at Tehran University. At least two students were killed, and many more beaten or arrested. The dormitory block was completely trashed.

With difficulty, Pegah turned the conversation to the march. The neighbourhood has been assigned a stretch of Azadi Street equidistant from Azadi Square and Enghelab Square. Who wants to be a marshal? The marshals are to wear scarves over their mouths to avoid recognition. The idea is to gather the marchers into groups as they arrive at Azadi Street. 'The *basijis* are like hyenas,' said Pegah. 'They pounce on stragglers. If enough people come, the groups will coalesce and it will be impossible for the *basijis* to attack.' She did not add, 'Unless they use live ammunition.'

Slogans against Khamenei are out, she continued. 'Our issue is not with Khamenei, but with Ahmadinejad and the manner of his election. Our demands are the annulment of the election and the holding of a new one. If we shout radical slogans we play into the hands of people who say we are extremists trying to topple the regime, and we'll drive away moderates. Our strength,' she went on, 'is the peaceful nature of the movement. You can be sure they'll be working their hardest to turn things violent. This mustn't be allowed to happen.'

Everyone looked at Mamad. He held up his hands and smiled. 'OK, OK, I can see the sense in that.'

Rumours have been flying. The Revolutionary Guard is split. A senior commander has been arrested for refusing to deploy his men against the protesters. The homes of other ideologically suspect commanders have been raided. The authorities are handing out tight *soosool* T-shirts to the *basijis* so they can infiltrate the march. Spies will be everywhere, shooting footage with their cellphones. 'These people should not be confronted,' said

Pegah. 'We are not doing anything wrong. The constitution allows us to march peacefully. It's a basic human right.'

On the morning of the march Mrs Abbaspour looks at Mohsen across the breakfast table and widens her eyes theatrically. Her husband doesn't notice; he is looking out of the window, as he does every morning, at the neighbour's cypress tree. She mouths the word 'clinic', with emphasis, then, seeing her son's puzzled look, 'blood test'.

Mohsen pours himself some tea and says loudly, 'Ma? Didn't you want to go to the clinic for your blood test today?'

Mrs Abbaspour nods and says, 'I thought I would, but I need someone to take me. You know how weak a blood test makes me feel.'

Mohsen says, 'That's all right, Ma, I'll take you. Around two, OK? Bring water in case there's a long line.'

His father grunts over his bread and cheese. 'I'd take supper, if I were you, considering the rate they get through patients at that clinic.'

After lunch, in a taxi on the way to Azadi, they pick up Amin and Solmaz and Solmaz's mother. The older women are glad of each other's company. They ask warily after their respective husbands, and it is clear from their answers that neither man has an idea that his wife is going to an illegal demonstration which the authorities have promised to suppress. Solmaz's mother says, 'There's something to be said for having a husband who doesn't care', and everyone laughs.

The car is approaching Azadi Street. It's close to three o'clock. Mohsen drops his mother and Solmaz's mother off at a fabric shop. They want to look at chair covers and then they will come down and march for justice. 'Call me when you reach Azadi and we'll meet up,' calls Mohsen as the women walk off. He, Solmaz and Amin go to Azadi Street. They reach the side-street they have been allotted. Pegah, Mamad and the others are there. Marshals are standing in groups at the top of the other side-streets, all the way from Azadi Square to Enghelab Square. There is no sign of the police or *Basij*.

Azadi Street is vast and desolate. Mohsen fears that the number of marchers will be fewer than anticipated, the hardline press and TV will show the demonstrators dwarfed by the street, and the movement will look feeble. He glances up at the unseasonal clouds. Amin asks Mohsen to tighten the knot on the back of the scarf that covers his mouth. Then Mohsen's eye is caught by a movement from the nearest side-street. Some people are coming into Azadi from this and other entry points. The marchers are arriving.

'Mohsen!' Pegah calls. 'Don't let them go any further into Azadi than where you are standing.' Mohsen and the others are corralling the marchers. 'Stay close to each other,' he calls, but already the number of people is growing and the separate groups that have formed at the entrances to the cross-streets are getting closer to each other.

From both sides, from north and south, thousands of people are entering the street – young and old, students and wasters, housewives, addicts, clerks, *soosools*, lovers. All wear green: face-masks, wristbands, T-shirts. Some have green face paint. Others carry green flags or slogans written on cardboard. By now two-thirds of Azadi's considerable width has been engulfed and no distinction remains between the different groups.

Mohsen tries to call his mother. The network is down. 'Solmaz,' he shouts, but Solmaz has been caught up by the crowd and can't hear him. Mohsen is reassured by the sight of other middle-aged women around him. The two mothers will be fine. A police helicopter circles overhead. As one, the people tip their heads back and ironically cheer the helicopter, which tips its tail bashfully. In the cockpit, Mohsen imagines, someone is speaking into a mouthpiece, saying, 'Yes, sir, millions!'

Pegah's eye catches his. Her eyes have narrowed; she is grinning through her mask. He grins back. 'Millions,' he shouts.

The Islamic Republic of Iran was formed out of crowds. Now, aged thirty, it manufactures them for important, symbolic dates. But it's one thing for the authorities to gather people, using buses and loudspeakers and the promise of a free lunch, for the anniversary of the revolution or in support of the Palestinians. For a crowd to sweat and pant, however, it must be pushing. It requires a fence or a wall to rub up against and eventually break.

The crowd starts to move slowly towards Azadi Square. Slogans swell. They wash over the crowd behind Mohsen and break two miles away at Enghelab Square. Mohsen starts walking, too, and Mamad appears at his side, handsome and disreputable in his green face-mask. 'They stole our votes,' the two friends chant, 'and now they're posing with them.' Another slogan comes: 'You are the chaff!' From a balcony overlooking the street an old lady flashes a V-for-victory sign from her wheelchair. The crowd cheer her.

Still, people pour into Azadi Street from the side-streets. To judge from their neat clothes, and the women's regulation black hoods, many of the newcomers are bureaucrats and private-sector employees. The working day is ending and they have come out with their colleagues to demand their rights. 'By the end of the week,' the people shout, 'Ahmadinejad will be gone.' They are smiling and laughing. They show affection and consideration towards the young and the old. There will be no petty crime in Tehran today. Khamenei can't ignore this, can he?

The crowd backs up. Mohsen goes up on tiptoes. He looks back towards Enghelab and ahead, to Azadi. The belt of humanity extends for several miles and soon it will take up the full width of Azadi Street, which is 200 yards across. Mohsen realises that he is a part of the biggest protest gathering Iran has ever known, and suddenly he feels himself to be a part of a much bigger body, one that has been demanding representative democracy for a century or more, and that now, here in Azadi Street, is coming of age.

Mohsen glimpses his *setar* teacher, Jalali, walking with his wife. Mohsen greets Jalali respectfully; he, in turn, is delighted to see his student. Jalali is old and slightly bowed, and he has come here in the knowledge that, if there is panic, a stampede, he will go under. He is a fine musician who has recorded with the masters of Iranian classical music, but he is also a progressive and a democrat, which brings its own price. Jalali's concerts have been cancelled. His compositions have sat for years in the Ministry of Culture and Islamic Guidance, waiting for clearance. Perhaps this is an Iranian perversity, Mohsen reflects as they part, that a gentle man who delights in culture and loves his country should not be raised up by the authorities and celebrated, but reviled, mistrusted and trodden underfoot.

Or Shamlu, that poet of freedom, losing his notes and his poems to the Shah's police, in and out of jail, ending his days in isolation and loneliness under the Islamic Republic. How many thousands of Shamlu's lines have yet to be published, for lack of a government permit? And yet this man did not succumb to the temptation of exile.

'My light is burning in this house; my water ripples in this jar; my bread is laid here.'

Mohsen is weeping privately now, as the raindrops fall and the crowd shouts, 'Greetings to Muhammad, the tears of God are falling!' He vows never to leave this country, never to drop his shoulders and abandon Iran to its fate. Some people are singing the unofficial national anthem, 'Ey, Iran!' and he joins in, misty with emotion. Suddenly Amin is alongside him. Amin too is gleaming, his forehead wet from the rain. He has removed his green face-mask and Mohsen does the same. Amin has seen Mohsen's mother, arm-in-arm with Solmaz's mother, smiling, giving the victory salute.

A massive cheer rises from half a mile, a mile back, and the word spreads that Mousavi is among the protesters, as he said he would be, and is now addressing some of the people through a megaphone. 'It's a nice surprise,' Amin says, 'when a reformist keeps his promise.'

A hundred yards short of Azadi Square the marchers see some *basijis* skulking in a side-street and chase them away. They chant a slogan comparing the brave and selfless *basijis* of the Iran–Iraq War with the animals of today. In the next side-street, prevented from doing their job by the vast crowd, sweepers sit on the pavement. The marchers extemporise, 'Street sweeper! Take Ahmadi with you!'

It's seven o'clock and the sky is turbulent when they get to Azadi Square and the fallen Shah's monument – a squat arachnid against the sky. The whole of this vast space, as big as Red Square, is a pageant of figures in green.

The marchers begin to disperse. Most of them head north, and this route becomes an unanticipated extension of the march. Mohsen is deliriously happy; the authorities' decision not to break up the march is a sign of weakness and indecision. The police presence has been confined to a few bemused traffic cops and the helicopters overhead. He recalls reading about the power of crowds in Eastern Europe when the Iron Curtain fell – how, when the despots were confronted by such crowds, they lost their will to live.

Mohsen and Amin are walking north and this is when the trouble starts.

The first inkling they have is a change in the tenor of the slogans. Something hard is being chanted ahead of them, something they can't quite make out. The people are repeating it, bullet-like.

They get closer and the slogan is clear: 'Death to the *basijis!*'

Mohsen walks faster. He wants to get closer, to see what is going on. Amin is at his side, his face blank with fear. From the counter-current of people who have turned around and are returning to Azadi Square, and some hurried snatches conversation of people as they pass – 'They've got guns up there!' – it's clear that a confrontation has started. Soon it will be dusk. The cloud is dog-black above them. They hear the first shots, the first screams.

Instinct tells Mohsen to break into a run and get closer. Instinct tells Amin to turn around and walk away. Mohsen grabs Amin's arm. 'Come on!' he says, trying to contain the excitement in his voice. 'Just a few seconds and then we'll leave.'

Ahead there is what looks like a normal house or apartment block; it must be a *Basij* barracks. Flames are rising from the fenced enclosure around the house, and a gun barrel appears at an open window. A hail of missiles is directed at the window and a man in fatigues scurries across the roof. The man comes as close to the lip of the roof as he dare, and fires into the crowd. Mohsen and Amin are too far away to see if anyone has been hit. The people react as in a concatenation, running this way and that. Then, a few moments later, they creep back towards the barracks and resume their stone-throwing. 'We will kill those who kill!' they shout.

Mohsen shouts, 'Death to the *basijis*!'

As the flames rise higher, Mohsen turns to a man standing nearby and asks, 'What's on fire?' The man replies, 'Some motorbikes, I think.' Now there are two figures on the roof, visible through the smoke, firing from the hip and dodging the missiles. The crowd is chanting, 'Don't be scared! Don't be scared! We're all together!'

Amin shouts, 'Let's go!' and tugs Mohsen's arm.

Mohsen is yelling, 'We will kill those who kill!' He turns reluctantly.

Amin and Mohsen start walking south again, away from the burning barracks. 'Let's get off the main road,' says Amin, and he and Mohsen enter a side-street heading east. The street has cars parked down both sides, but there is no sign of life. The two boys are parallel to Azadi Street, getting further away from the fighting. Mohsen is looking over his shoulder as he walks. The *Basij* barracks is obscured by other buildings, but he can still see the smoke rising into the sky.

'Stop!' Amin says suddenly. His arm restrains Mohsen. Six uniformed *basijis* are ahead of them. They are standing at the next corner. They are waiting for people who have come from the barracks. Mohsen remembers what Pegah said about the *basijis* being like jackals. The *basijis* are psyching each other up. Two or three of them are jogging on the spot. They are singing a *Basij* slogan: 'God is Great! Khamenei is our leader!'

They see the two boys. One of the *basijis*, a man of about forty with a salt-and-pepper beard, says something to the others.

The *basijis* are no longer running on the spot. They are looking up the street. Two hundred yards separate the *basijis* from Mohsen and Amin. The *basijis* start to run.

Mohsen and Amin run. They run towards the main road, which now seems like a refuge, with crowds to lose oneself in and welcoming pandemonium. Mohsen is running with long, easy strides, but Amin is no sportsman. As a child he suffered from asthma. He is terrified and this makes him pant all the more. Looking over his shoulder, worried that the *basijis* are gaining on them, he swerves inadvertently from the middle to the side of the road. Next thing he knows, he has slammed into the wing-mirror of a stationary van.

Amin drops to his knees. Mohsen stops and races back. He yanks Amin to his feet, but Amin is dazed. Blood pours from a big gash on his forehead.

'Get up!' Mohsen orders. Amin gets up, but he can't run. He is close to losing consciousness. Suddenly Mohsen notices a figure at the side of the street. It's a woman beckoning from an open door. 'Come in here!' she hisses, but Amin can hardly move, so the woman rushes into the street and helps Mohsen drag Amin across the street and through the doorway. She slams the door shut.

They are in a parking lot on the lower ground floor of an apartment building. Mohsen makes out the shadows of the cars neatly parked. It is dark and there is a smell of gasoline. 'Quick!' the woman says, 'There's a door at the back. I'll open it and you can get out.'

But Amin can hardly stand up, let alone run. He is groaning. Mohsen swears at him. 'Shut up! They'll hear you!'

The *basijis* are banging at the door. 'Open up, filthy whore!' They are trying to force the door with a crowbar. A young voice says, 'Maybe it was the next-door block.' Another, older voice replies dismissively, 'No! I saw them come in here. Look! One of them's bleeding.'

'Listen!' the woman whispers to Mohsen and Amin. 'Go and hide under one of the cars and don't come out. I'm going to leave the back door open, so if they get in they'll think you left by the back entrance.' The woman disappears.

Mohsen and Amin retreat to the darkest part of the car park. They crawl under a Nissan Patrol. Amin is panting like an old man. 'For God's sake,' Mohsen pleads, hugging him, 'stop making so much noise!' Mohsen can see the *basijis* through the metal grille of the door. Their faces are consumed by rage. There is the sound of grunting and exhortations to God and the Imam Ali, and then the hinge has been forced and they stand in the doorway. Mohsen wishes he had his truncheon with him. Amin is shivering.

'Where are you?' They come in, hitting the walls with their truncheons. 'We're going to take you out, apostate scum!'

'Where's the light?' the older one, the commander, demands. Someone finds a switch. The ceiling light is very feeble. The commander orders, 'You two! Start up at that end, looking under every car. We'll start at this end!' One of them has a match, but he burns his fingers looking under the first car.

'Ow!' The others giggle.

They are looking under every car in the place. They are coming closer to Mohsen and Amin's end of the car park. Amin's body is as stiff as a board. Mohsen is wondering when he should roll out from under the car. His eyes scan the floor for some weapon he might use. Suddenly, from the far end of the car park, one of the *basijis* shouts, 'Look!'

The others whirl around. 'What is it?'

'There's a back door!' He is disappointed. 'It's open. This is how they got away. They're miles away by now.' Someone hits the wall with his truncheon in frustration.

There is silence for a few moments. The *basijis* are catching their breath. Mohsen sends a prayer of thanks to the woman who let them in.

'You know what I'd like to do?' says another of the *basijis*. 'I'd like to catch that bitch who let them in and give her a going over.'

'You'd never find her,' another replies, 'she could have fled with them or else she's anywhere in the building.' The *basijis* are walking around the car park, squinting in the half-light, sizing up the cars. Peugeots, Xantias, Kia Prides. Cars they could never dream of owning.

From where he is lying, Mohsen sees the older of the *basijis*, the one with the salt-and-pepper beard, standing in front of a 206. He says, 'I have a feeling this car belongs to that cunt! Just a feeling.' He raises his truncheon over his head and smashes it down, obliterating the windshield. The car alarm starts to wail. He gives a whoop.

The mood has changed now. The other *basijis* are laughing. One says, 'No, brother! You're wrong. This is the one.' It's an older Paykan. He smashes in the windshield. The wail of the car alarm. A second smash. A second car alarm. And so it goes on. And in this way the three *basijis* go around the car park and smash in the windshields and the windows of every single car that is there, and the sound of the wailing, staccato, pulsing, long tortuous notes rises until Mohsen feels as though he is locked in the brain of a madman.

They lie there, in the shadows formed by the chassis of the Patrol, listening to the pulsing of the car alarms, until the *basijis* swagger out of the door and down the street, and then they pick themselves up and find the entrance to the stairs that lead up to the lobby of the building. The inhabitants of the building are slowly, gingerly coming into the parking lot to see what damage has been done to their cars.

Three more huge marches are held that same week, on successive days, along different routes in the capital. They are held in silence, partly out of respect for the dead, and partly for pragmatic reasons, for silent marching is conducive to the atmosphere of calm and non-violence that the movement is trying to foster. On Tuesday the protesters march in north Tehran and the route takes them past the state TV headquarters. Clashes take place after dark between protesters and the security forces, leading to the deployment of thousands of *basijis* who harass and arrest people and smash in the windows of passing cars. On Wednesday a west–east route is chosen, from Haft-e Tir Square to Enghelab Square, and on Thursday a route through the poorer south of the city. Each of these marches attracts several hundred thousand participants.

The city is in a joyous mood and the roofs at night are crowded with people shouting *'Allahu Akbar'* and 'Death to the Dictator'. In general, people gravitate to the bigger apartment blocks, where they can shout anonymously, from high up. Amin and Mohsen go to Mamad's apartment block and there, on the roof, some ten or fifteen families come together and shout their hatred and resistance into the night. Everyone is conscious of history. 'It's all to do with the code of kings,' says one man. 'The King cannot stay when the people hate him because he is concerned about his place in history.'

When the Council of Guardians starts investigating the complaints of the three losing candidates, and it's announced that a number of ballot boxes will be opened and the ballots recounted, some hope that the public pressure is having an effect, that the authorities are losing their nerve. But the view that most people have of the workings of the regime is partial, and the widespread reading of every official statement or position as an example either of disinformation or information designed to look like disinformation – the national tendency to interpret everything other than the way it appears – is an obstacle to a realistic reading of what is going on.

Why, a couple of days into the crisis, did Ahmadinejad delay his trip to Russia to address the Shanghai Group of countries? What message did he take, or receive, when he eventually went, a day late? Is there truth in the rumours that: a) the Russians, keen supporters of the Islamic Republic, trained the Revolutionary Guard in terror tactics, much as the Americans and Israelis did prior to the revolution; and b) the most brutal of the anti-riot policemen are Arabs on secondment from Hezbollah? Why does the BBC's Persian TV channel seem perversely keen to broadcast the voices of Ahmadinejad supporters? Is the BBC preparing to come down, as it has many times in the past, on the side of the regime?

As a people, the Iranians have access to the Internet, and they are eager to hear news of the outside world, and yet they have no direct experience of the outside world. Their analysis of international affairs is coloured by conspiracy theories and paranoia. They attribute immense cunning to people who are, in fact, quite simple. They subject a throwaway remark to laborious exegesis. Their goldfish-bowl perspective plays tricks on them. They regard their own country as the key to world prosperity, stability and civilisation. Narcissism takes hold. Obama, Medvedev and Sarkozy are preoccupied by Iran. Because Iran is so horrible, so beautiful, so old, so new.

The people's idea of time contracts. The nation's favoured units have traditionally been seasons, decades, centuries. Now things happen in an evening. Mousavi's wife, the radical-turned-moderate Zahra Rahnavard, announces that a march has been cancelled for fear of a violent reaction from the security forces. Numerous protesters indicate their intention to go ahead and march, with or without the politicians' support. This forces Mousavi's hand, and he announces that he will participate in the march, if only to 'calm the people'. This process, of statement, reaction and counter-reaction, takes a few hours.

Iranians are not used to conceptualising political and social development in this way. They like their decisions to be based on learning. They are being rushed. They are glued to the TV all night because the early-evening BBC bulletin may differ substantially from later ones. Across Tehran and other cities, the wee hours of the morning see unannounced visits by plain-clothes men who, without showing warrants or explaining who they are, take away reformist politicians and journalists. Ghoochani, Jalayepur, Hajjarian, Leylaz, Nabavi, Tavasoli – the list goes on. In the past, the arrest of any one of these men would have dominated the bulletins for a week. Now they are fillers between news that the authorities have stashed away the bodies of several martyrs in hospital morgues, and that Obama has come out in support of Iran's protesters, telling them, 'The world is watching, and inspired.'

Iranians discover that they have an ambivalent attitude towards technology. Cellphone cameras; Facebook; Twitter; the satellite stations; the media are supposed to reflect what is going on, but they seem, in fact, to be making everything happen much faster. There's no time to argue what it all means – what the protesters want, if they're ready to die. The movement rolls forward, gathering speed, and no one really knows where it's going.

Ayatollah Khamenei has an idea. Khamenei grew up in the seminary and he spent time in jail before the revolution. He knows what it is to sit and think, or pray, or study, for long periods. He knows what it is to devote oneself to understanding something, a work of Islamic jurisprudence or a poem, expelling all outside stimuli. This distinguishes him from Ahmadinejad, who stands on his own froth.

Khamenei may not be a learned theologian, but he is far from unintelligent and he delivers quite skilful speeches. Khamenei doesn't have a rapport with his people. They judge him not with their emotions, but according to his performance, which, of late, has been disappointing. Now he is caught between the embarrassment of a cack-handed fraud, his desire to appear impartial and statesmanlike (which comes from his considerable vanity) and the strongest impulse of any professional politician, which is to survive.

Khamenei's eyes are fixed on the Shah. Learned theses have been written about his demise. The Shah fell because he allowed the economy to overheat and ordinary Iranians were hit by austerity measures that followed. He offended national pride with his pursuit of Western values and his disdain for Islam. He fell because his American allies pulled the plug on him when they saw Khomeini waiting in the wings, and mistakenly believed they could do business with mullahs.

All these theories may have an element of truth, but for Ayatollah Khamenei there are other, more pertinent factors. The Shah fell because the impression he gave was one of indecision.

He made concessions not when he was strong, and could claim to be behaving magnanimously, but in moments of weakness, and this encouraged his opponents to make further demands. He could be pompous and violent, turning machine guns on crowds of his own people, for example, and that for any Muslim ruler amounts to joining the ranks of the unrighteous. Finally, the Shah was not very good at dividing his opponents. By the end, he had alienated people who would, in normal circumstances, have favoured him over the alternatives on offer.

Khamenei wants to control events, not be led by them. His aim is to be firm, but generous. He wants to be predictable, for people to be able to say, 'We know where we stand.' He condones violence, but asks that it be committed subtly and away from the public eye. Intimidation and fear are more his thing.

We are four days into a movement that seeks to right an accounting error. You might think that, in order to save the Islamic Republic, Khamenei would be prepared to sacrifice his protégé Ahmadinejad – that he would permit a rerun or quietly order a recount that would leave neither candidate with more than 50 per cent of the vote, necessitating a second round run-off between Ahmadinejad and Mousavi. After all, the country's reformist leaders have lined up and affirmed their loyalty to the Guardian-ship of the Jurist, the unique position that Khamenei fills, and which only Khomeini has filled before him. They want nothing other, they insist, than to work in harmony with him. They want to reform the system in order to save it, and that includes the sacred institution of the Guardianship of the Jurist.

The trouble is that everyone, on both sides of Iran's political divide, knows that this isn't the whole story. They know that if the Supreme Leader gives in now, it will be like the Shah's giving in, under pressure, and Khamenei will emerge from the crisis weakened, perhaps mortally so. They know that, for every Mir-Hossein Mousavi who professes his fidelity to the revolution and its precepts, there are ten younger supporters of Mir-Hossein Mousavi who feel no such fidelity. How, after this, could Mousavi build a cabinet of men who are loyal to the Supreme Leader? All would be suspect, and rightly so! How would a President Mousavi deal with the theologians Soroush and Kadivar, who, from overseas exile, have expressed their support for the separation of politics and religion, condemning the theocratic principle on which the Islamic Republic has been built?

Mousavi would certainly let these people back into the country. He would see to it that they got back their old chairs at the university and the seminary. They would write and say what they believed, giving voice to thousands who think like them, and it would only be a matter of time before Khamenei was asked to give up some of his powers, to make public his revenue sources, to relinquish his control over the Council of Guardians and the Revolutionary Guard. It would only be a matter of time before it was suggested that the office of Supreme Leader should be ceremonial, that he must act within the sort of constraints that operate upon, for example, Queen Elizabeth II of Great Britain.

Suppose, for one unlikely minute, that this is what Khamenei is resolved to do. He wants to ditch Ahmadinejad and bring in Mousavi. Would Ahmadinejad roll over and allow this to happen? No fear! Ahmadinejad is an ambitious man who feels the hand of God on his shoulder. According to a widely credited story, he once said of the Supreme Leader, 'Does he think I'm his president? I'm not his president; I'm the president of the Imam of Time.'

The president is well protected. His friends and family members are everywhere in the corridors of power, and in the Revolutionary Guard – which he has encouraged, through sham privatisations and fixed tenders, to take a grip on the country's economy. Finally, he knows a great deal, much of which must be incriminating or ruinous.

No, it would not to be easy to get rid of Ahmadinejad, even if Khamenei wanted to.

Mohsen receives his warning on June 16, the day after the Azadi Street march, as he is getting ready to go and join the second of the great demonstrations. The bell rings. The screen shows a woman in early middle age: Shadi. Shadi says quickly, 'I'm sorry for coming unannounced, but I have something to say in private.' She glances up and down the street, then nervously back at the screen. 'I need you to let me in now. I've been loitering for the past ten minutes waiting for the street to empty.'

Mohsen buzzes her in, telling her to come to the third floor. Shadi takes off her shoes at the door and he gives her a pair of slippers. He shows her into the kitchen. The morning tea is still stewing on the hob. Mohsen pours them both a glass. 'Can I get you something sweet?'

'Do you have any dates?' Shadi sits down without taking off her coat and headscarf. Clearly she means to say her piece and leave quickly. Mohsen puts some dates on a saucer and places the saucer on the table next to her.

'You don't have your cellphone on you, do you?' she asks, and he shakes his head. 'I keep my cellphone in my room.'

'Good. The reason I'm here is that they came to see me this morning, two of them, and they were asking about you.'

Mohsen has been expecting something like this since the night of the election, when he attracted the attention of the man in the white shirt by defending the Doctor. He has not, however, been prepared for the fear that now takes hold of him. With some difficulty he suppresses his rising sense of panic. He will not show his unease. Certainly not in front of a woman.

'Who were they?' he asks casually.

'I don't know,' Shadi says. 'From the ministry, I presume. When I asked for their ID cards, they said they were the anonymous foot-soldiers of the Hidden Imam. They started by asking some questions about me, but didn't bother disguising the fact that their main interest was you. The funny thing was, they didn't know what your name was. Either that or they pretended they didn't.'

Mohsen takes a large gulp of tea, scalding the roof of his mouth.

'What did they want? What were they trying to find out?'

'They showed me a photo of you inside the Doctor's surgery and asked me who you were.'

Mohsen nods. 'That would be the night of the election, when the first results were coming in and we all got together. There was a *basiji* who took photos of us all with his cellphone. But there were several men in plain clothes as well. I wonder if they were the people who came to see you.'

Shadi shrugs. 'I don't know. Anyway, I told them the truth – well, almost the truth. I said I hadn't been involved in the election campaign and that I'd only seen you once. Oh, yes – they knew about the meeting at Amin's house, and I said it wasn't a meeting, more a kind of social gathering. I said that you and I hadn't spoken to each other. In fact, I expressed complete ignorance about you!'

Mohsen is pale. Shadi holds up a date stone and says, 'What shall I do with this?' Mohsen indicates an ashtray on the kitchen table.

'Go on.'

'There's not much else to say. To be honest, I don't know why they came to me. Perhaps they knew I hadn't been a member of the Mousavi campaign and thought of me as a dilettante who might cooperate with them. Anyway, they said, 'We think this man may be using the post-election crisis to advance the agenda of the Hypocrites, and that he may be involved in terrorist activities.' They said you had made some incriminating statements during the raid on the campaign centre. It seems you had some kind of argument with the man who arrested the Doctor.'

'Hypocrites? Terrorism?' Mohsen cannot conceal his fear and bewilderment. 'What do they mean, I made incriminating statements? All I said was that the Doctor had committed no crimes!'

Shadi smiles gently. 'I'm just telling you what they told me. The main thing is that you should know they're on the lookout for you and may be in the process of gathering evidence against you. Or it might all be a red herring. Who knows? Sometimes I think they don't know themselves! In any case,' she goes on, finishing her tea, 'it wouldn't surprise me if they made further visits, perhaps even to you. If I were you, I'd be careful about what I said on the phone and about being seen with other people from the campaign. And I should get rid of anything here' – she gestures around her – 'that might be incriminating.'

'What about attending the marches?'

'I think you know the answer to that question, Mohsen. You know the marches are illegal and they're picking up people simply for attending them – not just the reformist bigwigs, but normal people like you and me. If you go out and they see you, or if you're captured on film, they might try and pin some outlandish charge on you. They might even make out you're some kind of ringleader. It wouldn't be worth it.'

Mohsen thinks for a few seconds. 'Do you think all this has to do with the Doctor?'

'I don't know. I asked them about him and they said I shouldn't worry and that he'll probably be free in a few days, but I don't trust them. I'm not sure these guys even knew where the Doctor is. They were trying to get my help and they wanted to give me as much good news as possible.'

Mohsen was puzzled. 'Help? What help?'

'They were sounding me out as a mole, someone they could use.' Shadi looks at her watch and gets to her feet. 'I'd better go now. Would you have a look down the street for me and see if the coast is clear?'

Mohsen gets up, but he finds himself wanting Shadi to stay. He prefers the idea of contemplating his predicament with her, rather than alone. He goes to the window, pulls back his mother's lace curtain and looks down the street. Two uniformed policemen stand at the far end.

Mohsen motions for Shadi to come to the window. 'They don't seem to be looking in the direction of your front door,' she says, 'but you never know. I think I'll sit for a few more minutes, if I may.' She takes off her headscarf and coat and drapes them over the back of her chair. She runs her hands through her thick black hair and says, 'May I smoke?' Mohsen nods and she withdraws a packet of Kents from her pocket. She said, 'When do your parents get back? They may be surprised to find me here.'

Mohsen frowns. 'It's got nothing to do with them.' He lights

Shadi's cigarette. Then he says in as conversational a tone as possible, 'So, were you at the march yesterday?'

In this way, for the next hour or so, over cigarettes and more tea, Mohsen and Shadi become friends. If they met a few weeks earlier, politics would have accounted for a small fraction of their conversation. Now, it seems unnatural to discuss anything else.

Mohsen immediately feels he can be critical. He criticises those people who supported the 1979 revolution and had a change of heart only when it was too late. Mohsen feels entitled to some words of penitence from these people, an acknowledgement of their mistakes; it's the young of this country who have paid the price.

Shadi shows little remorse. She takes a conveniently long view of Iran's democratic development. The revolution, although it disappointed her in many ways, was a stage along the way. In particular she dismisses Mohsen's argument that Khomeini and his supporters hijacked the revolution after victory was assured. 'You can forget that nonsense. I don't say this with any great pleasure, but when Khomeini's supporters came out into the streets, we breathed an enormous sigh of relief because it was the moment when the revolution went from being theoretically possible to being practically inevitable. It wasn't groups like mine or your father's which brought about the revolution. They laid some groundwork among the middle classes, but it was Khomeini who created the mass movement.'

Seeing Mohsen's frankly disbelieving expression, Shadi goes on, 'You may not enjoy hearing this, but if Iran is a religious society today, it was a thousand times more religious back then. It would have been impossible to mobilise the masses without the help of mullahs and Islamic imagery. The revolution was all about the martyrdom of the Imam Hossein and the caliphate of the Imam Ali.'

Mohsen turns the conversation to the present, where he feels more secure. 'But what's happening now isn't like the revolution. We aren't going into this with our eyes closed. We're not naive like you were.'

Shadi smiles gently. 'Well, that's pretty big talk, and I won't deny there's some truth in it. Yes, I agree, we have become more politically aware, and we'd never make the same mistake of turning a politician into a kind of demigod whose word can't be questioned. But you don't remember the first year of the revolution, before the Khomeinists took complete control. This country was freer than it had been ever before. You had all these different groups debating on TV. You could write and say pretty much what you wanted. When I see what's happening now, and remember what things were like back then, I find myself thinking I'd like to experience that kind of freedom again.'

Mohsen shakes his head vigorously. 'I've heard my father say this kind of thing, but freedom in this country has always been the result of some crisis or division at the top, and it's always been temporary. The Leftists swallowed the Khomeinists' lies about forming an alliance against Western imperialism. Then Khomeini no longer needed them and he eliminated them. As much as Khomeini and the people who came after him, it's because of the Leftists that we're in the mess we're in today.' By this, Mohsen means, 'It's because of people like you that we're in the mess we're in today.'

'Hold on!' Shadi is smiling. 'You seem to think that Iranian society was capable then of the same things it's capable of now. You can't judge Iranian society in the 1970s using today's criteria. Look! Nowadays we find former *Tudeh* members have social-democrat children! Today's demonstrations are full of women! When I marched with my sister back then in 1977 and 1978, our male comrades would encircle us to stop us getting hurt. That wouldn't happen now – women are taking responsibility for themselves. Can you imagine how important these changes are?'

Mohsen helps himself to a cigarette from Shadi's packet. He wonders what he would do if his mother suddenly walked in to find him smoking in her house with a strange woman. It's not something that has happened before.

Shadi leans back in her chair and says, 'Let me put this another way. Do you think democracy is possible if women don't achieve their rights?' Mohsen shakes his head. 'Well, back then, it was independence, not women's rights, that united people. After the revolution it was fear of a counter-revolution or American attack. Now, can you can guess how many men I saw in the anti-*hejab* demonstrations of March 1980?' Shadi sees Mohsen's puzzled expression and laughs.

'Of course! You've never heard of these marches! Why should you? Your father was a *Tudeh* member, and the *Tudeh* were no more interested in women's rights than the Khomeinists were. Well, I'll tell you! Imagine, Mohsen, we were out in the streets, thousands of women, protesting at Khomeini's ruling that from now on we should all wear the *hejab*. We marched for several days and they fired over our heads, and in the end we forced Khomeini to back down. Imagine! We forced Khomeini to back down and there was hardly a man among us!'

'Yes,' says Mohsen sourly, 'but he didn't back down for long. Compulsory *hejab* was introduced eventually.'

'Exactly! My point is that we women were on our own at the time. No one was helping us. There was no civic society back then. Even the most enlightened men didn't regard the *hejab* as their war to fight. Well' – she shrugged – 'the result is well known. Eventually, as you say, the *hejab* became compulsory and then they went a step further and insisted on the chador in public offices . . .' She stubs out her cigarette. 'I mean, you see the situation! Do you think we had a revolution for this?'

Mohsen shrugs.

Shadi goes on. 'And you blame us, as individuals, for supporting Khomeini! Of course, you're right, but you have to see things in the round, Mohsen. The revolution happened at the wrong time, before Iranian society even got its head around ideas like democracy and rights. Underneath all the talk of freedom and sovereignty we were all about old-fashioned things like virtue and pride. You have to admit that my generation has changed, and not beat up on us for having been different when we were young. You'll ask the same of your children!'

Shadi finishes her cigarette and peers out of the window. The policemen are gone. 'I must be off or I shall miss the march.' Standing at the door, she says, 'I don't think I'll come and see you for a while, Mohsen, but I hope our paths cross again in the future. Remember what I said, and be careful in the next few days and weeks. The Islamic Republic is very skilled at destroying young people who cross it too overtly. Don't become one of them.'

She leaves and he feels stronger, clear-eyed and defiant. He recalls Shamlu's devastating lines about Khomeini shortly after the revolution. Shamlu was one of the few who foresaw what the revolution would become.

> So beautiful am I,
> Only your 'God is Great' can describe me.
> I am a poison without antidote when exposed to you.
> If the world is beautiful,
> Flattery demands my presence.
> Half-wit!
> I do not oppose you.
> I deny you.

Mohsen's father has reacted in a curious way to the knowledge that his wife and son were out in an anti-government demonstration that turned violent and left several people dead. He has said nothing. Mohsen's father has worked so hard to wipe out his past, to mask his former beliefs and make a home for himself in this republic of lies, that he has been disconcerted by the rebirth of ideals.

His wife has been out demonstrating for the past four days on the trot. She returns, flushed and excited, and quietly makes his dinner without explaining why she is late. She is a petite woman, but this week she seems bigger, more substantial. Mohsen's father would like to find some way of letting her know that he could, if he wanted, simply order her to stay at home – but that wouldn't ring true. Mohsen's father has been forced to admit new complexities into a marital relationship that was, until the election, characterised by brutal candour on his part and slightly refractory submission on hers.

Amin hasn't attended the subsequent marches. He has been waiting for his head to heal and his stitches to come out – he doesn't want a truncheon-blow opening things up. Solmaz gives him an account of the previous day's march when she comes to his house each morning.

Mohsen gets his accounts from his mother, whispering in the kitchen while his father watches TV.

Mohsen cannot bring himself to throw out all his political books, so he leaves them in a corner of the janitor's cupboard behind the elevator shaft. He pours half a bottle of arrack down the sink. He drops the stolen truncheon into some bushes in a nearby park. He doesn't call anyone from the campaign.

One day Mohsen's mother gives him an envelope that Amin's mother passed on to her. It's a letter from Amin. Amin tells him to watch his step; they're watching you. Don't go on any of the marches. Stay at home and play your *setar*. Read poetry or masturbate! Mohsen burns the letter in the sink and washes the fragments away.

Mohsen tries Amin's suggestions, but applies himself distractedly. He cannot think about anything but the movement – the latest march, the latest statement by Mousavi or Karrubi. He asks his mother to buy some anti-filter software and spends hours on the Internet, getting the latest news from Facebook and the reformist websites. He cuts articles from sites that most people, not having anti-filter software, cannot access, and pastes them into round-robin emails for forwarding to friends and acquaintances.

Every morning he goes out to buy the newspapers and it's an opportunity to have a glance around and see if anyone is keeping tabs on him. Again there are uniformed policemen in his street, and again there's no telling why. He buys his newspapers and comes back home, spreads them over the kitchen table and reads them from cover to cover. One in particular, Karrubi's newspaper, is strikingly outspoken in its news and comment, but then the leaders of the Islamic Republic are no longer united, and disunity furnishes gaps through which audacity can leak.

He reads every item, whatever the subject matter, for its possible political effects. Each disappointing piece of economic news – and there are many, even if Iran has so far avoided the recession that has blighted the developed world – strengthens his hope that the disgruntled masses will be drawn into the protests. The Tehran municipality, he reads, has plans to turn Vali-ye Asr into a largely one-way street. Mohsen wonders if this is designed to facilitate troop movements. Then he wonders what effect it will have on the shopkeepers, whose ability to bring in stock and attract customers will presumably be curtailed. He is aware that, up to now, the bazaar and most of the poor have been observers of events. He is sensitive to the government's charges that this is an uptown movement, a movement of the middle class.

He keeps the radio on all day and watches the main TV bulletins on state television, BBC Persian and the Voice of America. He follows with scepticism the partial recount of ballots, sensing that this is a ploy by the authorities to buy time and that the election results will ultimately be endorsed. He watches as Ahmadinejad tells the leaders of the Shanghai Group of countries, including China and Russia, that America is 'enveloped in economic and political crises, and there is no hope for their solution'. Ahmadinejad proposes a common currency for the bloc's consideration. He urges common action to counter terrorism. This, as Tehran is paralysed by demonstrations. This, as the Islamic Republic tears itself apart.

How will it end, this life-or-death struggle in the tatty palaces of the Islamic Republic, where Rafsanjani and Ahmadinejad try to destroy each other and Khamenei whisperingly urges on his favoured contender? Mohsen remembers the cunning, murderous President Rafsanjani of the 1990s. Rafsanjani has become one of the good guys, and Mohsen supports him with the reluctance of someone who has no alternative.

Then there are the old men of Qom, ayatollahs who have expressed their horror at the attacks on university dormitories and the deaths of protesters. For the past three decades, these men have looked the other way whenever they have been shown evidence of official brutality. No longer. They realise that the prestige of the clergy will be destroyed if they are seen to be colluding in the barbarisms of a military dictatorship. In parliament, deputies daring enough to speak in favour of Mousavi receive punches and denunciations: 'Death to opponents of the Guardianship of the Jurist!' Everyone makes out that he is scandalised by 'unauthorised' attacks on the universities, but it's well known that these attacks could never have happened without approval from high up the chain of command.

On the foreign front, Britain is getting it in the neck. Manuchehr Mottaki, the foreign minister, has accused the British of dispatching planeloads of troublemakers in the run-up to the election. Mohsen, who shares his compatriots' loathing for Britain, which has spent the past 200 years meddling in Iranian affairs, is happy to believe the worst of the Brits. But he finds it hard to credit that the respective governments of Britain and Iran are engaged in a serious dispute. Like the majority of his compatriots, he believes that Britain is in a sinister pact with the Islamic Republic.

On the surface, of course, they remain antagonists. The BBC's Persian service has thrown the state broadcasting company into a tizzy. No one watches the official bulletins any more; the people are glued to the BBC. It's slick and believable and the presenters are articulate and well turned-out. It's everything state TV is not. It's the closest thing Iran has to a national channel everyone can be proud of, and it comes from London.

The authorities have been working overtime to scramble the BBC signal, but the crafty Brits are a step ahead, changing frequencies and flipping satellites. Iran's jamming signals are rumoured to be carcinogenic.

In professional terms, the official broadcaster's response to the crisis has been inept. State TV alternately belittles the demonstrations and talks up the heinous destruction that 'rioters' and 'hooligans' have wrought on public and private property. One channel describes Monday's monstrous pro-Mousavi march as a unity rally by the supporters of all four presidential candidates. A second channel ignores it altogether. According to a third, the greatest challenges facing the Islamic Republic are the provision of traffic cops in time for the forthcoming vacation season and the smooth holding of university entrance examinations.

Mohsen is furious whenever state TV uses Muhammad-Reza Shajarian's version of the revolutionary anthem, 'Iran, O Palace of Hope', as a backdrop to footage of Ahmadinejad and his triumphant supporters. Shajarian isn't merely Iran's finest classical singer. He is part of a generation of anti-royalist artists who put conscience and patriotism into notes and rhyme. His rendition of the *Rabbana*, the Arabic verses that greet the evening breakfast during Ramadan, transports Mohsen to the fasting months of his childhood and to his pious old grandmother sitting on the couch, fingering her beads and mouthing from the Holy Book. Now Shajarian is being violated, his art lowered by lying images. Didn't Stalin use composers this way?

In this way, sitting at home, listening, watching and reading, Mohsen spends much of that week. There are no more warning letters, the man in the white shirt does not come, and gradually he allows himself to believe that his panic may have been exaggerated. He is observing his mother, too, watching her rise. She is asserting herself through brisk activism over a sour, still husband. He wonders if it's the case that now, as the balance of power shifts on the streets, the balance in other households is changing as well.

On Wednesday evening there is to be a truce. The streets are silent and Mohsen and his father, like fathers and sons across the nation, have taken their places in front of the TV before the big soccer game, Iran versus South Korea, in Seoul. Everyone is watching – the protesters, the *basijis*, everyone – and they are willing an Iranian victory. For ninety minutes there will be a release from politics.

But things do not turn out as expected. Gradually, at different times, after the Iranian team emerge from the dressing room and strip off their tracksuits and stretch, as they line up to sing the national anthem, at some point during this process the people of Iran realise that an extraordinary thing is happening. No fewer than five of these handsome athletes, men who are not known as political activists, are wearing green Mousavi wristbands. They have taken Iran's internal politics to a Far Eastern soccer field. Whatever happens tonight, whoever wins, the headlines tomorrow will have nothing to do with sport!

Imagine the consternation in the state TV building! It's common practice for state TV to broadcast images from international soccer matches with a delay of several seconds – this allows them to edit out images of scantily dressed female fans or men swigging beer. But delays won't help here! Karimi, the captain has two wristbands! Whenever he comes into the frame his green bands glint and shine like emeralds. The commentators are being told: 'For God's sake don't mention the wristbands!' It's a scrappy first half and Iran's performance is bitty and inconsistent, but the Iranians go into the half-time break a goal to the good.

'We're going to South Africa!' Even Mohsen's dad is grinning.

The five players in question are not wearing their armbands after the break, which suggests that the half-time pep talk concerned subjects other than sport. They will be disciplined when they get home. (The Iranian Football Association will take the unprecedented step of consulting FIFA, the world governing body, about suitable punishments for players who take politics into the sporting arena.) The Koreans equalise after eighty minutes, and the result is 1–1 at the final whistle.

Iran isn't going to the World Cup. In normal circumstances Mohsen would be devastated, but now he is surprised to find that he hardly cares. Iran's sporting failure doesn't seem important next to the stunning political victory of Karimi and his brave comrades.

Not only sport, but culture, too, is being taken over by politics. The great Shajarian writes a letter to the head of the state broadcasting company, a man appointed by the Supreme Leader. In it he demands that the nation's TV and radio stations desist from playing his compositions. Shajarian's letter is short, and it is written in the maestro's own hand – he's one of the country's best calligraphers. It's like 1978 all over again, when Shajarian and his fellow musicians boycotted the Shah's TV company. It shows that, if you belittle and smother people enough, their feeble plea reverberates like a lion's roar.

Mohsen's week of inaction will come to an end on Friday, June 20. It is one week since the election, and it feels like a year, so laden with significance is every passing instant. Again, on this day, but this time with his mother and father, Mohsen sits down in front of the TV. Again, the streets outside are quiet. The reason is that Ayatollah Khamenei is to deliver the most important speech of his life, at Friday Prayers. The conservative press has described the event as an opportunity for the Iranian people to renew their vow of fealty to the Leader of the Revolution. The reformists hope that he will address their concerns and propose a way out of the mess. The spouses of some of the political prisoners clearly hope for their husbands' freedom. But Khamenei is not a miracle-worker. He is a politician.

Mohsen sits down as the camera pans over an expectant congregation, sitting under the vast awning at Tehran University. The congregation is the usual mix of time-servers, paid loyalists and genuine ideologues. A young albino, ashen against the darker faces around, holds a youthful photograph of Khamenei above his head. 'The omens are not good,' says Mohsen's father. He is alluding to some significant absences in the VIP section at the front. There is no Rafsanjani, no Mousavi, no Karrubi and no Khatami. The reformist big guns are staying away, Mohsen's father warns, because they know what's coming. Mohsen's mother sits on a chair on her own. She has crossed her legs and is leaning forward, biting her lip.

Khamenei appears now, standing above the congregation, framed by a flimsy arch with prayers inscribed on it. He has an injured left hand from when the enemies of the revolution tried to assassinate him, and it grips his notes like a vice, his right picking and unpicking at the hem of his gown. He begins speaking, softly, calmly, licking his lips between phrases in a way that makes you want to pass him a glass of water. He uses felicitous phrases. He is congratulating the Iranian people on the famous victory they scored over their enemies in the recent election, which is evidence for the special regard that the Creator and the Hidden Imam have for them. He is making them feel good about themselves.

Here is Khamenei, the head of a fractious family whose every member he loves, praising each of the candidates for the services he has rendered the Iranian nation and the revolution, castigating the country's foreign enemies for depicting what is happening as a fight between revolutionary and counter-revolutionary, when it is nothing of the sort. It would certainly have been better, he says, if the candidates had been less frank in their criticisms of one another. They have gone too far, he suggests, and overstepped the bounds of decorum. It's not right, for instance, for the president to be depicted as a superstitious lunatic. Ahmadinejad is sitting there cross-legged in the front row, rocking slightly on his haunches, gazing innocently at the Supreme Leader, looking like a superstitious lunatic.

Several minutes into the sermon, no one can be sure how things will end. 'What's going through his mind?' Mohsen's mother whistles. Mr Abbaspour replies, 'Don't pay any attention to that! Most of him is hidden underwater.'

Mohsen's dad turns out to be right. Khamenei's niceties are mere preliminaries, designed to establish his moral eminence. He has three main points to make. The first is that the election results were not fraudulent, the second is that Ahmadinejad is the lawfully elected president and enjoys his full support, and the third is that Iran will not allow the West, Britain in particular, to go unpunished for interfering in Iran's affairs. These countries, Khamenei scoffs, 'imagined that they can bring about a velvet revolution with a few tens of million dollars of investment by a Zionist businessman, as they have in some small countries'.

Khamenei is on home territory, and his speech is repeatedly interrupted by a familiar series of slogans.

Death to America!

Death to Israel!

Death to Britain!

Death to opponents of the Guardianship of the Jurist!

Towards the end of his address, Khamenei's voice thickens. 'I am worthless,' he tells his congregation, 'I have a flawed body', and 'what self-respect I possess, which you gave me, I have here and will sacrifice on the road of this revolution and of Islam.' He goes on, imploring the Hidden Imam to 'pray for us, for you are our master, you are the master of this country and of this revolution'.

The audience before him, many of whom saw service in the Iran–Iraq War, veterans of one of the bloodiest conflagrations of the late twentieth century, know what they are expected to do, and that is dissolve into sobs at the delicious poignancy of the situation. In no time at all everyone is wailing and hiccoughing with emotion, waves of love and pathos lashing their bodies – including the generals and ayatollahs and judges in the front. Khamenei himself is affected. He dabs his eye with his good hand, and his voice falters noticeably.

Mohsen's father chuckles. 'He's weeping, the old fox!'

Mrs Abbaspour shakes her head. 'Do they have no shame?'

Mohsen is wiping his eyes. Not out of love for the Supreme Leader, but out of hatred and fear. Khamenei's warning is stark and unmistakeable. He orders the movement's organisers to end the protests. If they do not, 'Responsibility for the chaos that follows will be on their shoulders.' Pressure of this kind, he goes on, will not bring concessions. Accommodating illegal demands, he goes on, is nothing less than 'the beginning of a kind of dictatorship'.

It's decision day for Mohsen. Last night, from the *Basij* barracks in the next alley, came loud cries as the militiamen psyched themselves up. 'Death to the Hypocrites!' they shouted. Some of their slogans drew inspiration from Khamenei's first name, which he shares with the Imam Ali. 'We are not the people of Kufa, to leave Ali to his fate!' In the seventh century, the people of Kufa abandoned Ali when his enemies grew too strong; they are a byword for fickleness of heart. To listen to their slogans, anyone would think the *basijis* were the underdogs, the embattled unarmed ones!

Mohsen and his parents drink their breakfast tea. No one discusses what is going to happen. How many will die today? Contradictory rumours have been swirling. The Revolutionary Guard have deployed tanks on the outskirts of Tehran. Today's march has been cancelled by Mousavi. To which there is a water-tight answer: it's not Mousavi's to cancel.

Mohsen glances slyly at his mother. She is being more civil to his father than she has been over the past few days. Mohsen would not be surprised if, in private, his father has tried to dissuade her from taking part in the march. From her happy, determined expression he knows that she will go. After his father goes out of the kitchen, Mohsen turns to his mother. 'Don't go today, Mother dear. Today will be different. They'll shoot today.' She doesn't reply. Her back is facing him. She's doing the washing up. 'Ma!' he demands. 'When was the last time you ran? I mean, really fast?' He sighs. 'You don't even own a decent pair of sneakers.'

Then he thinks, his heart pounding, 'Today is the day we write our destiny. If I am not there, how can I call myself an Iranian?' He says to his mother, 'We'll go together.' She turns around from the sink, her lips pursed.

They go at lunchtime, but not before she has been out into the street to check if anyone is watching their front door. 'Don't bring your cellphone,' Mohsen says, 'or anything that might iden-tify you. If you drop it, they'll pick it up and arrest you later.' Mohsen and his mother walk quickly to Vanak Square and catch a shared taxi going south. They are going to her brother, Bijan's. The other passengers and the taxi-driver glance warily at each other. Everyone knows what's going on – that the taxi is taking people to do battle with the Islamic Republic.

The traffic is going by outside, but the street corners are filling with small detachments of *basijis*, four or five to a street corner, standing around in their small groups. Mohsen feels hatred and fear. His mother feels it too. He whispers, 'Ma, I'm begging you, get out at the next square and catch a taxi home again. This won't be the place for you.' She smiles, as if to say, 'I wouldn't miss this for the world.' But she's rubbing her hands, which is what she does when she's nervous.

Mohsen's Uncle Bijan is the assistant manager of a bookshop in a covered passage of shops near Enghelab Square, where the demonstration is supposed to start. Most of the shops in the passage are shut. The lights in Uncle Bijan's shop are on, but he is alone; his last customer left before 11 a.m. They sit at the back of the shop, behind piles of books, and Uncle Bijan brings them tea and biscuits. 'I just spoke to a friend who lives near Laleh Park,' he says, referring to a park where the demonstrators have arranged to meet before making their way to Enghelab. 'The park is packed with *basijis* and riot police. They're driving people back into the streets around.' It's obvious the security forces are determined to prevent the marchers from achieving critical mass. 'If enough people don't get through to Enghelab Square,' he says, shaking his head, 'we don't stand a chance. The *basijis* will be able to pick off the smaller groups of demonstrators by one.'

There is a rap at the bookshop's plate-glass window. Uncle Bijan gets up and runs round the piles of books to see who it is. Mohsen and his mother hear him speaking to someone at the door, and then he comes back. 'That was a *basiji*,' he says, 'telling me to shut the shop and go home. I told him I'd be out in a few minutes.'

'Do you think he'll come back to check?' asks Mohsen's mother.

Uncle Bijan shrugs. 'I don't know, but I'd prefer my boss not to come in tomorrow morning and find the windows smashed and his books destroyed! I think what I'll do is lock the door and turn out the lights and we can slip out when we want to.' Uncle Bijan gets up again, shuts the shop and comes back. 'From now on, we only whisper.' There is just enough light to read by. Mohsen picks up a novel. Mohsen's mother and Uncle Bijan are conversing in low tones. He is trying to persuade her that the march is no place for a middle-aged woman, and that she should stay here in the shop. She says, 'Bijan! If you don't cut it out, I'll go there on my own with my mask on and then we'll see what happens!' Suddenly Uncle Bijan raises his hand for quiet. They hear the sound of boots against the floor of the passage outside. It's the *basijis*, come to check if anyone is still around. 'That's it,' thinks Mohsen, 'this is the moment when we become illegal.' The sound of the boots recedes.

A little later, Uncle Bijan says, 'Listen!' They fall silent. They hear the distant sound of chanting. It's coming from the street outside the passage. Bijan creeps to the door of the shop, unlocks it and looks down the darkened passage into the street outside. He ducks back into the shop and whispers, 'Come on, quick! The people are marching past the entrance! Let's go and join them!'

Mohsen grabs his mother's hand and they walk rapidly out of the shop, into the passage and into the sunlit street. A group of protesters, about fifty of them, are marching down the middle of the street, which meets a bigger road, which in turns leads to Enghelab Square. The protesters are wearing green and flashing V-signs and shouting '*Allahu Akbar!*' Uncle Bijan calls, 'Put on your face-masks!' Mohsen looks briefly at his mother, with her shining, terrified eyes and her green face-mask. Then he too starts shouting, '*Allahu Akbar!*'

They march in this way for a block or two. This section of the street is residential and a few people come out of their front doors as they pass and attach themselves to the group. The more people who join, the greater the marchers' security, but at present the group feels perilously thin. The sidewalks are filling up with local residents, mostly women and children and old people. Some of them shout blessings as the marchers pass. 'May God protect you!' Other residents lean out of their windows to get a better view, and the demonstrators urge them to come and join in: 'You won't get your votes back by staring out of the window!'

From the affluent, well-scrubbed appearance of many of the people around him, Mohsen guesses that they have come from north Tehran. Others are more cheaply dressed – swaggering young men from more modest neighbourhoods. Most people in the group seem to be taking instructions from a short, muscular man with a greying beard and blunt, pugnacious features. Mohsen hears someone address him as Haj-Agha, which people often use when speaking to a mullah; his shirt flaps over his trousers, *Basij*-style, and he is old enough to be a war veteran. There are no more than five or six women in the group and this makes Mohsen feel apprehensive for his mother. With one hand she holds his. With the other she gives the V-for-victory sign.

Suddenly someone bounds out from among the people at the side of the road and says to Haj-Agha, 'We've got a bunch of riot police waiting in the next alley.'

'Which side of the road?'

'The right side.'

Without breaking stride Haj-Agha orders everyone to move across to the left-hand side of the road and get ready to turn back if they have to. But the people at the front of the group have almost reached the main road and are lengthening their stride; they are keen to get to Enghelab Square as quickly as they can. 'We'll be less exposed there,' shouts one man. 'We need to get into a bigger crowd.' The group has lost its compactness and some of its members, a middle-aged couple in particular, are falling behind. Haj-Agha calls to those up ahead, 'Not so fast! Wait for the others to catch up.' Then Uncle Bijan looks back over his shoulder and exclaims, 'Good God!'

Mohsen follows his gaze. A group of about twenty riot police have appeared behind the group and are in pursuit. They move awkwardly in their black body armour, and from behind their visors comes a muffled, ominous chant. The people standing at the side of the road realise the danger and start hurling abuse at the riot police. They shout, 'Murderers! Have you no shame!' From an upstairs window a woman screams, 'Don't hit them! Don't hit them! They're Iranian, just like you.'

The cops are getting closer. The middle-aged man in the group has lagged behind; the leading cop catches him up and yanks him backwards by the collar. The man falls heavily to the ground and writhes in agony as the cop hits him with his truncheon. Mohsen shouts, 'Haj-Agha!' Haj-Agha stops in his tracks. He and Mohsen and several others race back to try and save the middle-aged man, who is now being kicked and beaten by three cops. The man's wife is screaming and clutching her head.

Suddenly, as he runs, Mohsen feels a sharp pain on his shin. Sitting in a doorway, he raises the leg of his pants and sees that his calf has been nicked by something sharp. 'What happened, Mohsen?' It's Uncle Bijan, panting, at his side. A few paces behind he sees his mother, pale from the emotion, covered in sweat.

Further up the street, behind the cops, a group of local boys have gathered and are hurling fragments of brick and other missiles at the cops' backs; a piece must have spun off and struck Mohsen in the leg. The cops seem in two minds now. Some are intent on chasing the original group of protesters, while others turn to confront the stone-throwers. A roar of anger surges through the people watching on either side of the road. 'Death to the *Basij*!' they scream. Some of them step into the road and start advancing towards the cops. Further up the street a dumpster is on fire; smoke rises into the sky.

This section of road is full of broken bricks that have sailed over the cops' heads. Several car windshields have been smashed by wayward projectiles, and the sound of tinny car alarms fills the street. Mohsen and some of the others start picking up the fragments and throwing them back towards the riot police. A woman pleads, 'Don't play their game! Don't you see they *want* violence!'

Mohsen carries on throwing, feeling with pleasure the pull on his shoulder, watching his missiles shatter on the asphalt; you have to talk to these people using a language they understand. It feels to Mohsen as if he has strayed into TV footage of stone-throwing Palestinians engaged in street-battles with the Israeli army. Mohsen has grown up with such footage. It's part of the Islamic Republic's iconography. And now the Islamic Republic is Israel.

Mohsen's mother is by his side, screaming at the riot police.

Her face is dark and distorted with anger. 'Animals! You dare hit your fellow Iranians? You DARE?'

Haj-Agha has reached the middle-aged man and is helping him up. The man's pants are covered in blood and his wife is clutching her head and sobbing. At that moment a policeman rushes forward, his truncheon over his shoulder. Haj-Agha stands up to face him. The policeman has raised his visor because of the heat and his face is visible: a normal, lived-in, Iranian face. He notices Haj-Agha's appearance, that of an old-style revolutionary, and is momentarily floored. He stops in front of Haj Agha and shouts, 'Get out of the way! It's not you I want! It's the Hypocrite on the ground!'

Haj-Agha is staring fixedly at the cop. Haj-Agha is withdrawing his hand from his pocket, but it holds not a knife but a laminated card. It's Haj-Agha's injured veterans' card. It shows how badly he was injured in the war with Iraq. The card was given to him by a grateful nation; it embodies self-sacrifice and revolutionary virtue. The cop looks away. He doesn't want to see the card. Again he shouts, 'Get out of the way!' but he has lost his ardour. Haj-Agha says softly, almost tenderly, 'What are you doing? Do you know what you're doing?'

The cop's comrades have retreated. One of them is about to fire off a tear-gas canister. 'Get back!' they shout. 'Get back!' Gratefully, he turns and runs to join them. The next thing Mohsen knows, his eyes and throat are burning, his nose is full of mucus and he's doubled up in the street.

'Take this!' Uncle Bijan shouts, handing him a lit cigarette. 'Water!' Mohsen mumbles, waving the cigarette away. Uncle Bijan replies, 'Water makes it worse.' He blows smoke from the cigarette into Mohsen's face. Mohsen sits down heavily on the sidewalk. 'Calm down!' Uncle Bijan commands. 'Breathe in the smoke.'

Mohsen sits in a doorway for a few minutes, inhaling the smoke from his uncle's cigarette. Gradually his eyes stop watering and it gets easier to breathe. 'They only had time to pop off one canister before they ran off,' says Uncle Bijan. The cops have escaped down a side-alley and the street is in the hands of the protesters. The number of burning dumpsters has risen to three or four. Several young men survey the field of battle, picking their way through the debris, raising their hands and giving the victory salute. A trickle of cars has started to flow, heading south–north. The drivers sound their horns and the protesters take on the role of traffic police, guiding the cars around dumpsters that they themselves, a few minutes ago, helped set on fire. The people are chanting a new slogan, coined after the Supreme Leader's tearful performance at yesterday's Friday Prayers: 'Pathetic Dictator! Crying won't help you now!'

Haj-Agha's group of protesters is dispersing. Some of the younger men drift off towards the Imam Hossein Square, in the east. Others are trying to return to the north of the city; two get a lift with a passing car. One of the women protesters is sitting on the kerb, weeping softly. A second has her arm around her. Haj-Agha is kneeling on the ground. His face is red and his body convulses as he coughs. 'He must have been gassed in the war,' a man says sympathetically, patting him on the shoulder, 'and now he's being gassed by his own side!' Someone is binding the bloody leg of the middle-aged man who was beaten by the riot police. The beaten man's wife stands over him, wringing her hands, repeating, 'O God, let them only receive their just deserts!'

Mohsen can't stop grinning. They put the cops to flight! He has taken part in a great victory.

Suddenly, from the direction of Enghelab Square, he hears the sound of gunfire. There is a second, underlying sound – a mechanical murmur, getting louder. He says, 'What's that?'

Uncle Bijan replies, 'It sounds like motorbikes.'

A man and a woman, residents of an apartment block looking onto the street, are pressing the middle-aged man and his wife to be their guests for a few hours. 'Your husband is in no state to walk,' the woman tells the man's wife. 'They only need to look at him all bashed up and they'll realise he was in the demonstration and arrest him on the spot. You can stay with us and have something to eat, and then my husband will drive you home when things have calmed down.' The middle-aged man and his wife gratefully accept. Haj-Agha declines a similar offer, even though his coughing is persisting. His wife will be worried. He should be getting home.

It turns out that Haj-Agha lives quite close to Mohsen's family. 'My car is about ten minutes' walk,' he says. 'We can go there together and then I'll drive you home.' His face turns red and he clutches his sides.

Two young men on a moped skid to a halt nearby. Immediately several other people come up and engage them in conversation. Mohsen hears the word 'Enghelab'.

Mohsen goes across to the group and says, 'What's the news from Enghelab?' One of the young men turns to him and says breathlessly, 'We've just come from there. We were lucky to get away. The *basijis* have overrun the square. There are thousands of them. They came on their bikes. They've driven the people into the streets and alleys and they're going after them. You wouldn't believe it; it's pandemonium.'

'Are they shooting live ammunition?' Haj-Agha asks.

'I saw them shoot live ammunition as well as tear gas and pepper gas,' the young man replies. 'You know this pepper gas? It burns the skin. It hurts like hell. People are talking of at least twenty deaths. They're carting off the arrested people to the Labour Ministry in Azadi Street. That's where they've been refuelling their bikes. These choppers' – he indicates a helicopter, circling overhead – 'are telling the *basijis* where there are concentrations of protesters, so they can direct their forces.'

The people standing around the motorcyclists look blankly at each other. One man says, 'It's over, right?' His voice is slow and sad. 'How many people lie dying in this city – right now?'

Haj-Agha rouses himself. It's a huge effort. 'Hold on!' he says. 'We knew all along they wouldn't just say, "Be our guests! Come and have your protest today!" The moment Mr Khamenei opened his mouth yesterday, at Friday Prayers, we knew this much. OK; it's time to go home now and lick our wounds. But I'll tell you this: they're really scared. I've never seen them this scared.'

Haj-Agha swallows hard. He has the little group's attention. He forces himself to go on. 'Do you think this is the only street the protesters control? No way! *This* is what we need to do, not storm the state TV building! We tie down huge numbers of police and *basijis*, we paralyse the city; the whole world watches on the edge of its seat!' Haj-Agha suppresses another coughing fit. He turns to an older man and says, 'Sir! You know the truth of what I'm saying. These kids will listen to you. Tell them to use their heads, not to get arrested, not to get hurt. The movement goes on! Don't you agree?'

Mohsen listens carefully but he's sore. It's not a victory, after all. Part of him longs to exclaim, 'Of course you speak with authority on these subjects. You brought Khamenei and the rest of them to power. You were a goddamn *basiji*!' But something in Mohsen admires Haj-Agha. He didn't see Haj-Agha throwing stones today, but he saw him stand up to a cop who could have smashed in his brains. He remembers what Shadi said, about the different generations maturing.

Uncle Bijan says, 'Let's get out of here before the *basijis* arrive.' Haj-Agha nods. His coughing has subsided. He urges the residents of the street to go indoors. 'No more confrontation – that's my advice.' He gestures at the young men around him. 'You're no use to anyone if you're in jail or in the morgue.'

The four of them start walking westwards. Mohsen feels less confident. The *basijis* will arrive soon to take back the lost territory. Trying to distract himself, Mohsen engages Haj-Agha in conversation. 'You don't look like a typical protester.'

Haj-Agha smiles evenly and says, 'I'll tell you what a typical protester looks like. He looks like someone who's had enough of all the lies.'

Haj-Agha expresses surprise that Uncle Bijan allowed his sister to come out on the protest. Mohsen's mother says, 'You're obviously feeling better, Haj-Agha! Without the involvement of women, this movement would have never have gotten off the ground.'

A little further on Haj-Agha says, 'You see the intersection?'

They see it, about half a mile away. 'We only need to cross that and then my car's a bit further on. We could take a different route, through the side-streets, but it would make our journey much longer and there's no guarantee the smaller streets won't be full of *basijis*.' The others offer no opinion. They trust Haj-Agha. They walk on. Closer to the intersection Mohsen hears the same low roar, of *basiji* motorbikes. There is a second sound, over the top of that: the sound of people chanting.

'What are they chanting?'

Uncle Bijan frowns. 'I can't make it out.'

They are closer now. They are trying to make out the chant. Now it is clear.

'Death to Khamenei!'

They approach the intersection. The figures of the protesters and the shapes of the cars that are stuck at the intersection become firm, real. The chant continues – a drill, the beating of wings, something terrifying and unstoppable.

'Death to Khamenei!'

Only ten days ago, this was a slogan one didn't dare think, let alone utter. Now it's been released and is growing, filling the town. These people aren't just calling for the death of one man. They're calling for the death of the Revolutionary Guard and the *Basij* and every corrupt official that has ever addressed his fellow citizen with uncouth, seraphic pieties. It's death to the public executions and the sanctioned wife-beatings, the morals police and Chavez and Putin and all those thugs in the world who call themselves friends of the Islamic Republic. It's death to the past thirty years. It's death to fear.

'Death to Khamenei!'

Mohsen and his companions have reached the intersection. There must be 300 pedestrians milling about, chanting, and twenty cars sounding their horns and the carcass of a motorbike burning in the middle. The people have gathered around this carcass. The fire casts a flickering light over a huge mural of a celebrated martyr.

The four stand this side of the intersection, wondering how

to get across. Uncle Bijan nudges Mohsen. 'Basijis,' he says. Mohsen follows his uncle's gaze. The basijis are arriving from the south, two to a bike. Those riding pillion dismount and stand, fondling their truncheons. A man in plain clothes is among them, in dress and demeanour not dissimilar to Haj-Agha. This man raises a loudhailer to his lips and addresses the people over the din.

Mohsen and Haj-Agha and the others are some fifty yards from the man, and can hear what he is saying. His tone is thoughtful and conciliatory. He reminds the people that this is an illegal gathering and an inconvenience to normal people trying to go about their business. He asks people to go home before he is forced to disperse them. As he speaks, quite unexpectedly, he turns and looks in Mohsen's direction. Mohsen says, 'Good God!' and realises with horror that he is no longer wearing his face-mask. He must have ripped it off after the riot police fired the tear-gas canister.

The man in the white shirt is not wearing a white shirt today, but Mohsen has no doubt it's him. He knows the chubby cheeks and calloused forehead and the set, determined jaw. For a moment the man's quizzical gaze commands his. The man in the white shirt is trying to work out where he has seen this fellow before, but he can't devote himself to the question because he's responsible for a troop of basijis. Eventually he turns his attention to the basijis, who have begun advancing towards the protesters.

'Death to Khamenei!'

One of advancing basijis falls to the ground, clutching his knee. To judge from the reaction of his comrades, looking around and up, the missile came from the roof of a nearby building. More missiles follow; the basijis scatter this way and that. They are scared and angry and they hit anyone in their path. A group of women shriek, 'Animals!'

By now the basijis are among the cars, smashing windshields and dragging people out and calling the women whores and threatening to fuck them and their sisters. For a moment Mohsen forgets the danger. He is furious that his mother should be exposed to such language.

Two paramedics are trying to lift an injured man onto a stretcher, but the man is resisting because he knows he'll be arrested as soon as he reaches hospital. He screams in pain and fear and a group of people come and hustle away the paramedics, and he gets to his feet and stumbles away.

Haj-Agha is trying to guide his little group across the intersection to relative safety. He picks a path through the *basijis*. They could be beaten or arrested at any moment, but Haj-Agha gives the *basijis* his sternest stare as they pass, and they naturally assume he's one of them. Mohsen is terrified for his mother. Suddenly he sees a lanky *basiji* running towards him, trippingly, incoherently, fury written over his features. Mohsen braces himself, but the *basiji* runs past. He is chasing another young man wearing a green T-shirt.

Having crossed the intersection, the party starts walking quickly away. They get to Haj-Agha's car. His window has been smashed in and his stereo stolen. 'Accursed *basijis*!' he exclaims, before deactivating the alarm, and they get in.

It takes them three hours to get home, their progress impeded by small street-fights and diversions. On several occasions they pass *basijis*, who tell them to wind up their windows because of the tear gas. Sometimes the *basijis* look threateningly into the car and Mohsen looks back at them. He doesn't flinch from their gaze because he doesn't want them to think he's scared.

4

The people feel sad after June 20. They grieve for the fullness of the days that went before, and hunger for them to return. No one will forget where they were on June 20, what they wore, how they ran.

One woman, a heavy, mildly arthritic woman who should have stayed at home that Saturday, slipped and fell into a shallow water channel while waddling away from the *basijis*, and in her terror the sides of the channel became insuperable walls. As she flapped, waiting for the *basijis* to catch up and smite her, an angelic young woman materialised and pulled her out to safety, and the older woman felt the warmth of the younger woman's hand in hers for days to come.

Solmaz and Amin were close to Neda Agha-Soltan when she died in Kargar Street. They were close enough to glimpse a frozen tableau of people kneeling, craning, prognosticating over someone on the ground. During the coming days, time and time again, along with millions of other TV viewers around the world, they saw Neda's eyes, as white as death, and the blood trickle from the corner of her beautiful mouth, down her cheek and onto the road.

The following day four friends met at the apartment of a woman with a cure for every ill and smoked opium from a pipe and recited poems and were petted by the woman until their bodies were free of impurity and they tripped from the barren present into a brilliant, gem-like past.

> When silver decrees that gold should be worshipped,
> And lies become the umpire of every bout,
> When the air, the air I breathe, life-giving air,
> Becomes a death mask for countless hundreds –

Tehran stops in those days after June 20. The banks open in the morning; of the customers, there is no sign. Bureaucrats turn up to their offices, rearrange their desks and go home. Computers are untouched, envelopes unopened, light-bulbs unchanged. The roads are dead, the rush-hour funereal. Commercial transactions are put off. To listen to music, to exercise one's right to smile, to work up an appetite – there is something indecent about these things.

'I can't seem to think of anything other than last Saturday,' people say. 'I feel drained of energy.'

For a while the foreign channels torment the people with images of that day. Then, from a great distance, picking up on Iran's inertia and bewilderment, they allow the crisis in Tehran to fall from the summit of the world's news agenda. How long was it there? Two weeks? Three? Not long enough.

The state has won time. Now it must act to limit the damage. Sense must be made of events, a simple story written for the people to swallow without thinking. The achievements of the Ahmadinejad years, Iran's progress towards the status of a regional power; these must not be obscured by local difficulties. The story is made in the offices of the Supreme Leader and the president, by the state broadcaster and editorialists at the pro-government newspapers *Kayhan* and *Iran*, by judges, generals and spooks.

Either Mir-Hossein Mousavi and Mehdi Karrubi have been duped, or they are genuine believers in the cause of godless Western imperialism. They stand at the head of a fifth column of atheistic liberals and counter-revolutionaries who hate the

Islamic Republic because it is holy and pure. They are Zionist-loving Hypocrites, or perhaps monarchists in disguise. They are guided by Britain, Iran's old neo-colonial foe, with Israel and the countries of the European Union in satanic attendance. As for the United States, whose new president says he is ready to parley with the Islamic Republic; behind the smiles, the United States has not given up its enmity towards the Islamic Republic. That much is clear from Obama's recent words, his unabashed self-identification with the rioters and hooligans.

One of the pro-government sites gives prominence to an article in which a distinguished Principalist reminds readers of the venerable prophecy that the demon Dajjal will begin his plotting against Islam in the time of the Hidden Imam. He postulates that Israel is Dajjal and that people like Mousavi, who follow the orders of the West, are in the armies of Dajjal.

Over the coming days the official story is frenziedly propagated through statements, television and radio broadcasts, and in articles in *Kayhan* and *Iran*. British diplomats are expelled for their 'role' in the disturbances, which apparently extended to ferrying planeloads of troublemakers into the country before the elections. The Brits respond in kind and there is talk of the Islamic Republic downgrading relations with the nations of the European Union. At the next Friday Prayers a scowling ayatollah urges the people to rally against the foreigners, 'whose sharp devilish teeth are ready to pillage the inheritance of your martyrs'.

The authorities deny accusations that they used excessive violence while putting down the protests. The demonstrators were only fired upon when they tried to storm a barracks with the intention of arming themselves. Many of the deaths were caused by protesters shooting each other, with a view to implicating the authorities before the court of world opinion. The *basijis* are a byword for innocence and submissiveness. As for the death of Neda Agha-Soltan, which has so exercised counter-revolutionaries and their allies around the world – it is as plain as night follows day that this is a plot.

The story-tellers furnish different, even conflicting details. Neda was shot by her own side masquerading as *basijis*. The film of her death was too aesthetically pleasing not to have been expertly choreographed. She was shot at the instigation of the BBC. Her death bore the hallmarks of a CIA plot. The monarchists were involved. No! It was the Hypocrites! Actually, Neda Agha-Soltan was not killed at all; she is living pleasantly in Europe.

The scowling ayatollah is more frank on the subject than perhaps he intends. He says, 'If the regime wants to confront someone, it would do so in a main road – why do it in a quiet side-street? In a quiet street they would arrest her, not kill her.'

What we see here are the palpitations of a group of men who are ill at ease in the modern world. A decade ago cellphone cameras did not exist, and anyone toting a bulky camera in a Tehran street could be quietly arrested and his images destroyed. Now everyone has a cellphone and almost every cellphone has a camera that can be used to record events during a demonstration. Back home, the images are uploaded and sent around the world.

A decade ago an insolent rant against the Supreme Leader delivered in front of a few hundred people caused a temporary stir – no more. The critic would be arrested or hounded into silence, and the rant would live on for the few hundred who had heard it, and their associates. Now, by contrast, the few hundred have cellphone cameras and they post clips from the speech on YouTube. Before you know it, the clips have received 100,000 hits and commentators at the foreign channels are analysing furiously.

The protests have been put down, but a flotilla of deeply incrim- inating images and commentary has sailed west. Here, after all that effort expended on blaming Neda's death on the enemy, is a medical doctor who tended in vain to the dying woman. He got on a plane and went to London, and here he is, speaking live to BBC Persian, flatly contradicting the official version of events. This man will not be able to return to Iran while the Islamic Republic stands, but he has thought things through. His conscience has told him to go public with what he knows, and he will face the consequences.

The instinct of the state is to shut everything down. Crash the cellphone network, close the Internet, confiscate a hundred thousand satellite antennae. But much of this technology is even more integral to the state than it is to the opposition. It would be hard to run the country without it. Then there is the question of a public image. What message do Iran's leaders want to give out – that they are terrified, panic-stricken? The official broadcaster is forever telling viewers that life in the capital is returning to normal. It's incumbent on the other organs to reinforce that message.

In the days following June 20 the state increases restrictions on the Internet and telecommunications, but tries to do this without paralysing the country. The authorities wage an unacknowledged war against BBC Persian, scrambling signals and raiding apartment blocks for dishes. Text messages can't be sent, and it remains virtually impossible to make foreign calls even from a landline. In most areas of the capital the Internet is even slower than usual, and access is blocked to thousands of sites. These measures are not announced. They are implemented and the people apply themselves to work around them. They pass around anti-filtering software. They go online in the dead of night, when the Internet works faster. They spend time outside Tehran, where the restrictions are less effectively applied.

All this is symptomatic of a wider, philosophical problem. When they embraced the communications technology of the West, the administrators of the Islamic Republic reassured themselves that they could do so without embracing its values. They did not realise that these values are embedded in the technology itself. Speed, the principle of unfettered access to raw information; free communication through a medium, Skype, which is hard to tap – these are as much an enemy as the polemics themselves.

Would it be possible, in today's Tehran, to commit a massacre along the lines of Tiananmen Square? It seems unlikely. The Chinese were able to suppress internal discussion of the massacre partly because there were no cellphones or Internet, and partly because China's rulers are more efficient dictators than their

Iranian counterparts. An Iranian Tiananmen would be immediately and widely publicised. It must be avoided.

This is what Iran's leaders are telling their thugs, their wild animals. Remember world opinion, the *basiji* reminds himself as he wades into a group of female protesters. Remember YouTube. Strike parts of the body that bruise, not those, like the skull, that are liable to split. Aim your rifle over the people's heads. Of course there are mistakes in the excitement. People are killed. It's inevitable.

One of the characteristics of an effective dictatorship is that its leaders speak with one voice. This is not something we get here. Iran is trying to jettison the democratic parts of its make-up and become a dictatorship precisely at the time when it is least equipped to do so. The revolution is being rent asunder. Even Iran's hand-picked, loyalist parliamentarians loathe the president, and do all they can to embarrass him. Increasingly we find supporters of Khamenei insisting publicly on the necessity of obeying the Guardian of the revolution as you would the word of God. We rarely heard such things in Khomeini's time. There was no need.

The Supreme Leader is perhaps the ultimate victim of technological advance. Thanks to the foreign channels and opposition websites, the people have got used to hearing him being referred to as plain old 'Mr Khamenei' and not 'His Excellency the Supreme Leader of the Revolution'. His actions are subjected to impertinent analysis, and his instincts, for self-preservation and power, picked over. It seems increasingly hard to return Khamenei to the throne he occupied. How can the representative of God also be a dithering politician who makes mistakes and orders his henchmen to attack their compatriots?

Mousavi and Karrubi have surprised everyone with their bravery and stubbornness. They carry on issuing indignant statements attacking the security forces and the government, and they remain alive and free. Every day, some senior official or newspaper columnist calls them fifth columnists and advocates their arrest.

Both men have children and other relatives who are under immense pressure. The authorities long to eliminate these two traitors, but fear a popular explosion. Although the people are admiring and respectful, they are getting more cautious. The number willing to come out into the streets has shrunk. Fewer people are willing to risk life and limb.

Some changes are being made to the way the protests are staged. From now on the demonstrations will be smaller, but more confrontational. An advantage may be gained by hiding the protests behind a screen – a pretext, ostensibly legitimate, for the people to come into the streets. Luckily, the calendar of the Islamic Republic is studded with such occasions: religious holidays and the birthdays and death anniversaries of imams.

The first of these anniversaries falls on June 28. On this day in 1981 the Hypocrites blew up the Islamic Republic's first chief justice, Ayatollah Beheshti, besides a further seventy of the great and the good. It's a useful pretext, for Beheshti is afforded much reverence by the Islamic Republic and the anniversary of his and the others' deaths is an occasion for mourning ceremonies. The occasion is full of ironies, for at the time of his death Beheshti was widely regarded as Khomeini's heir-apparent. What sort of Supreme Leader would he have made? Better than Khamenei? A comparison between the two men's sons is instructive. Khamenei's son Mojtaba is friendly with the Revolutionary Guard, helped Ahmadinejad come to power in 2005 and allegedly has eyes on the supreme leadership. Beheshti's son, on the other hand, is one of Mousavi's close aides.

Since June 20, Mohsen has been repeatedly visited by troubling memories of that day. His store of such memories keeps being added to by satellite television and YouTube. On occasion, he becomes confused as to whether a given memory is his or someone else's, or whether he and someone else witnessed the same scene. He sees violence in his dreams, and he sees the Doctor. In his dream he is sitting next to the Doctor in a crowded bus. Suddenly the Doctor's seat is empty and, although the bus is full to bursting, no one wants to sit in the empty seat.

Mohsen realises that he is more nervous than at any time since the elections. He is scared of what is happening to those of his friends and acquaintances who have been arrested. They number five, including the mother of a friend who was on her way to the family court to file for divorce from her husband and got picked up by some *basijis* on suspicion of going to participate in a protest. And he is scared for himself, for he senses that the man in the white shirt, having seen him at the intersection, in the midst of the fighting, may again be thinking about him.

At 8 p.m. on June 20, half an hour after Haj-Agha dropped them home, Mohsen's mother went to her room. The following morning she emerged, red-eyed and reeking of cigarettes. Mohsen's mother is the kind of woman who can't stand the sight of a sheep being sacrificed or a chicken's neck being wrung. Something ended for her on June 20.

The violence and chaos have finally made Mohsen's mother think that any dictatorship is better than not knowing who will die tomorrow, whether the city will go up in flames. She mourns for Neda Agha-Soltan, and the dead *basijis* too. 'They have mothers, as well.' She thinks of herself on that day, baying for the blood of her enemies, and is ashamed. She begs Mohsen to promise he won't attend another demonstration. Mohsen dutifully gives his word, but she doesn't believe him.

A few days later she asks Mohsen, 'Would you like to go abroad with Amin?' Mohsen is surprised by his mother's words because it's supposed to be a secret that Amin has decided to go. Amin's plan is to go to Istanbul and throw away his passport, and smugglers will hide him in a boat bound for Greece. Mohsen's mother has obviously been talking to Amin's mother.

'Amin,' she continues, 'has relatives there, established in the building trade.' Mohsen's mother is embarrassed to speak in this way. Her eyes run from his. She and Mohsen's father have set aside a sum of money. 'It's not much, but it's yours.'

Mohsen knows what being 'established in the building trade' means. It means getting up at five in the morning for the privilege of receiving half the minimum wage, slaving to pay off your debt to the smugglers, and at the end of it all there's no guarantee you'll be able to stay.

He says to his mother, 'I'll think about it.' He's cut up. Cut up because the money on offer will come from the fund his parents have set up for their old age. It hurts because this is their way of saying they would prefer to have him off their hands. But something in him wants to be off their hands. Doesn't freedom mean happiness?

The following day Mohsen goes to see Amin. He bumps into Solmaz as she comes out of Amin's house. She's borrowing a book, she says lamely, holding it up and smiling through her tears. Then she realises she's incriminating herself, for it's a book that will help her in the forthcoming university entrance test, and she looks away. Mohsen remembers her vow not to take the test for as long as Ahmadinejad remains president. 'What about the general strike?' he longs to demand. 'What about the boycott of all government institutions?' Solmaz looks shitty without her lipstick.

Everyone's parents are devising ways of persuading their children to give up their dissident activities. He pictures Solmaz's mother, sitting on the end of the girl's bed, saying, 'You think those politicians – that Mousavi, that Karrubi – would do anything for you? How come they're at liberty when everyone else has been locked away? Hasn't it crossed your mind that they're making an ass of you and will ride you into the ground to reach their destination?'

These other parents are like Mohsen's mother. June 20 changed them. They urge their children: don't back the losing team! Would you like to be barred from university and a career in the public sector? Do you think the reformists will provide for you and your family? Find you a spouse? Solmaz's parents are keener than ever for her to attend university, but this isn't because they particularly want her to have a career. They want her to be out of trouble and they want her to be marriageable. Everyone knows a degree increases your chances of a decent match.

Mohsen sits for a while with Amin, watching him take precious things out of his bag because he needs to travel light. Out comes his bulky edition of the *Shahnameh*, the nation's epic – in goes an abridged version.

'They could tell me to get going any day now,' Amin says. 'If you want to come, you'd better make up your mind.'

Mohsen leaves Amin's house. He walks the streets he has known since he was a child. If he goes with Amin, he thinks, he won't be able to take his *setar*. His shelves of poetry. He would hate to lose his identity – isn't that what happens if you move abroad? Above all he would hate to know that he had been defeated by Ahmadinejad.

He walks, preoccupied, saying curt hellos to anyone who greets him. Then he sees a familiar figure striding in the other direction. It's Shadi. He thought of her often on June 20, and asked after her in the days that followed. He's pleased she wasn't hurt or arrested. They engage in small talk. Shadi says, 'I'm going to see someone now. Would you like to come?'

He shrugs. 'Fine.'

They walk a few blocks, talking of this and that. Shadi has a few days off from her job in a government department. She's thinking of spending a couple of nights with her parents up in Rasht, on the Caspian Sea coast – 'If the conditions allow,' she adds. They stop in front of a modest apartment block and Shadi rings a buzzer. A woman answers. Shadi says, 'Haleh, I'm with my friend Mohsen', and they are let in.

A woman wearing a headscarf ushers them into her apartment on the first floor. The entrance is dark, but a spotlight shines on some framed photographs that have been arranged on a small table near the door. The Doctor, Ali-Reza, on a bridge some-where overseas. The Doctor, much younger, with more hair; the Doctor getting married to the pale, distracted woman called Haleh who has just let Mohsen and Shadi into her apartment.

They sit down around a small dining table in one corner of the sitting area and the woman whose life has been frozen answers Shadi's questions about her baby who is on the way. 'It's a boy.' Her eyes light briefly when she says this. Otherwise they are dull.

Mohsen says, 'Amin's sister's going to have a girl in a few months.'

Shadi says, 'Tell.'

Haleh has spent the past two weeks looking for her husband. Her mother-in-law has been staying, but she went back to Karaj this morning to look after her husband, the Doctor's father. From now on, Haleh's sister will accompany her whenever she goes out to try and find her husband. Haleh glances at her watch. It's OK. She has two hours before she should meet her sister and go to the Revolutionary Court.

Shadi drinks from the glass of tea that the Doctor's wife has given her and, inclining towards Mohsen, says, 'Mohsen was involved in the campaign with the Doctor. He was the one who objected when they arrested the Doctor, and he almost got arrested himself.' Haleh looks again at Mohsen. It seems to him that while she would like to show appreciation, sadness is the only emotion her eyes can express.

Shadi goes on, 'I bumped into Mohsen in the street and invited him along, as I knew he would like to meet you.' Mohsen nods gravely and Shadi adds, 'Anything you say in front of me you can say in front of him.'

It turns out that Shadi has come to see Haleh so she can take notes and send them to a friend in the US who is associated with an organisation that publicises human-rights abuses in Iran. Mohsen learns that Shadi has been trying to persuade Haleh to go public for several days, but she has resisted, fearing that this will prejudice the chances of her husband being released.

'Did anyone threaten you?' Shadi asks. The authorities have been intimidating families who go to the press with reports of abuses. Some families have been prevented from holding funerals for their children who were killed by the security forces, in case the funerals become an excuse for more protests.

'Nothing yet,' she says.

Shadi has a pad and a pen. She will write down what Haleh says and type it up later and send it to her friend in America.

Mohsen wonders what will happen if, as seems likely, Shadi's email and telephones are being monitored.

The Doctor is not one of those front-rank reformist politicians and journalists who have been arrested. His photograph isn't continually in the reformist papers alongside an affecting open letter or reminiscence by a wife or sister. The Doctor is one of dozens or hundreds of ordinary men and women who, from a position of relative obscurity, have now been eclipsed. He is missed here, in his surgery, in the grocery store, but nowhere else.

As the Doctor's wife speaks it becomes clear that she and her mother-in-law have travelled the length and breadth of the capital in search of her husband. They have joined up with other families in similar positions to write letters to the head of the judiciary, the intelligence minister and the president. They have pleaded with lawyers and sat outside the offices of important men. The Doctor's mother has shrieked and fainted on the steps of the Revolutionary Court. Again and again, they have prayed for the baby not to be born an orphan.

'I told them,' she says, 'I begged them! I said, "It doesn't matter if you don't want to release my husband, but just let us know, for the love of God, that he's alive!"' They went to all the police stations, all the hospitals. They were shown photographs of men in detention and men who were dead.

When she has nothing to do, the Doctor's wife calls his cell-phone, again and again, for an hour or two at a stretch.

They were outside Evin Prison on the afternoon of June 20. 'We had no idea about the demonstration that day. All we were thinking about was Ali-Reza. Then they started bringing in new detainees in those minivans with the blacked-out windows, and we asked the guard what was going on and he thought we were being facetious and told us to get out of his sight.'

The two women asked some of the other people outside Evin what was going on, and they learned about the trouble down-town. The Doctor's mother looked at the vans bringing hundreds of new prisoners into the compound and sobbed, 'How will we find him now?'

The following day they showed his photograph to someone who was being released from Evin, and he swore he'd seen Ali-Reza. They went home happy that day.

On the eighth day a nice-looking man at the Revolutionary Court went away for an hour, and when he came back he smiled gently and said, 'Your husband is to be released tomorrow. Go home and wait for them to call you, to let you know how much bail you need to post. You may want to prepare clean clothes in case his are torn or dirty.'

They rushed home. They begged bail contributions from friends and relations. They prepared a bag with all their love. They sat and waited. They repacked the bag. There was a flurry of telephone calls from other members of the family. 'Can't talk now,' they said, 'we're waiting for news.' They sat all night.

After two days they went back to the Revolutionary Court and tried in vain to find the nice-looking man. He was posted away, someone said. His mother is ill, said someone else.

Someone with a name very similar to the Doctor's was on the list of detainees that was pinned to the wall of the Revolutionary Court. They enquired loudly, with ill-concealed excitement, thinking it was a typographic error. 'The man with almost the same name as your husband is my son,' a woman told them. 'He's coming out today, please God.'

The following day, when they went back to Evin, an official in plain clothes told them that if a detainee has not contacted his family, it means he is being held in a secure unit. When they asked for more information the man said, 'These units are nothing to do with us' and turned his back on them.

The Doctor's mother screamed, 'So where should we go to bang our heads now? The Intelligence Ministry? The Revolutionary Guard? The office of the Supreme Leader?'

The man turned round and shouted, 'Get out! You'll get no answers if you show no respect!'

The Doctor's mother started shrieking. 'Did I say anything wrong? Did I insult anyone? Who are you to torture us in this way?'

The Doctor's wife hustled her from the room. 'In God's name be quiet, or we'll never hear from Ali-Reza again.'

Yesterday the Doctor's wife went on her own to the Revolutionary Court. She saw a line of parents applying for their children to be released so they could sit the university entrance test. She joined the line and said, 'My husband is a medical doctor. He has regular patients who need him. He needs to be considered under this scheme.'

They gave her some forms to fill out. A man standing near her whispered, 'You're wasting your time. If you haven't heard from him by now, he's in Kahrizak for certain.'

'Kahrizak?' Shadi and Mohsen say it together.

Haleh nods. 'I didn't know it either, but I do now – thanks to the gentleman in the Revolutionary Court. It's outside Tehran, in the desert. It's where they put all those drug addicts and hooligans they rounded up a couple of years ago. They treat them worse than animals. They keep them in cages and do unspeakable things to them.' She is sobbing now.

Now Shadi and Mohsen remember. The police staged a big operation. They arrested hundreds of addicts and pimps and other hooligans and beat them up and humiliated them in public. Then they took them away. Few ordinary citizens shed tears for these people. They little thought that their own children might meet a similar fate.

Haleh is exhausted. She is wiping her eyes with one hand and rubbing her unborn child with the other. She goes off to wash her face and they hear her blowing her nose.

Mohsen and Shadi talk in low tones. 'I'm surrounded,' Mohsen confesses, 'by people who think it's all over.'

Shadi shakes her head. 'That's quite wrong. If you consider the distance we've travelled in the past two weeks . . .' Suddenly she smiles her even, radiant smile. 'When we look back on all this in a few years' time, it won't surprise me if we say the stolen election was a blessing for this country!'

Mohsen rubs his chin. 'We went out to get the election annulled and we couldn't even manage that.'

'Fine,' she says quickly. 'I agree. We know Khamenei isn't going to suddenly order Ahmadinejad to resign. But look at the price they're paying! We've got ayatollahs who are famous for being cowards and are coming out and criticising the regime. We've got university professors resigning, dozens at a time. The Islamic Republic is split down the middle, and all kinds of Hollywood celebrities are issuing supportive statements from the other side of the world!'

Shadi folds her notes and puts them in her bag. Mohsen is struck again by her strength and optimism. 'You know,' she goes on, 'the amazing thing is not the number of people who say they won't demonstrate, but the number who will. Take my mother. She says to me, "Don't breathe a word to your father, but tell me when the next protest is and I'll be there!" We have a code. She phones and asks whether today we should go to the new Adidas store or not. That means, "Is there a protest today?"'

They laugh.

'Seriously, Mohsen, we've really got to them. They don't have unlimited resources, you know. The *basijis* get tired. They only have the energy for so much brutality.'

'Has anyone been asking about me?' Mohsen is dreading the answer.

She shakes her head. 'I've not been approached, and to the best of my knowledge the other guys from the campaign haven't, either. I'm telling you; they're preoccupied with other things!'

Haleh is back in the room now. Shadi takes her hand, presses it and declares, 'Look at this marvellous woman, so strong and brave.' She gazes at the Doctor's wife, who is smiling weakly, and says, 'He's going to get out soon. I promise.'

'I spoke to someone who lives near Mowlavi Street,' Mohsen says, 'and he said you don't hear a single *"Allahu Akbar"* down there at night. How can we succeed without the working class?'

Shadi laughs. 'Thus speaks the son of a Marxist! Forget all that stuff about the working class, Mohsen. Iran is now a middle-class, urban society, and all these people hate Ahmadinejad. The working class will join when it's time.'

Shadi sees that Mohsen is still sceptical. She goes on, 'You really should have a little faith. I can tell you, the revolution started much more slowly than this. It took months and months before all those people eventually came out into the streets. What we've achieved in two weeks, the revolution took a year or perhaps two to achieve.'

Shadi's words come back to Mohsen later that day as he surveys his half-packed bag. 'My place is here,' he says to himself, 'not throwing up off the coast of Greece.'

5

When he was younger Mohsen went to calligraphy class. He was quite good, but his teacher bore a grudge against him for refusing to fast in Ramadan, and the following term they told him the class was oversubscribed and he would have to go elsewhere.

Now Mohsen finds some green paint and a brush and inscribes in cursive *nastaliq* those lines of Shamlu that he loves, onto a strip of white cotton. It reassures him to think of the classical musician Shajarian as a fine calligrapher, of Nasser ud-Din Shah as a decent poet. Even the last Shah, dangerously self-educated, lusting after newness, found room in his ministries for men of depth and erudition. Where are they now? One minister bit another man's cheek in an argument. The culture minister is a former editor at *Kayhan*. The top ranks are packed with men who have the blood of dissident thinkers on their hands.

When Mohsen analyses his loathing for the Islamic Republic, he finds himself returning to its contempt for a thing of beauty. Forests are destroyed. Coastlines, rivers and verges are crusted over with trash. Cyrus the Great's tomb is sacrificed for a dam, and ancient arts and crafts casually made obsolete by a flood of cheap Chinese imports. A commissar interrupts a singer who dares perform the wrong song. Iran's most creative modern musician, a man who does falsetto, nonsense-poems and Kurt Cobain, is driven into exile.

Every year hundreds of thousands of Iranians go abroad, intending never to return. Most are young and many of them go on to live successful lives in the countries they settle in. The authorities are glad to see the back of them. It upsets Mohsen to think that he may become a part of this conspiracy to impoverish the country.

He needn't make his decision yet. Amir's plans have hit a snag. The Turkish and the Greek authorities launched an operation and some of the smugglers were arrested. Now everyone has to wait for the situation to calm down. It could be weeks before Amin gets the call.

'Come on!' Mohsen says to Amin. 'Let's go to the Beheshti commemoration!'

The movement has been pruned, but it remains green and living. It's becoming less about the election and more about ambitions for freedom that haven't been precisely defined. On the Beheshti anniversary a mullah named Ghaffari calls Khamenei a liar in a speech, and accuses him of discrediting the clergy. Mohsen is thrilled. Having never dared imagine a world without the post of Guardian of the Jurist, he and Amin now discuss its abolition. So insistently have the authorities evoked the 'threat' of a velvet revolution that they have feared it into existence.

The security forces will no longer allow large numbers of people to gather in such numbers that they are a menace to public order. The *basijis* want that monopoly for themselves. The protesters come together in small groups, ostensibly citizens minding their own business, going about their normal routine. Suddenly they coagulate and find their voice. 'Death to the Dictator!' Small protests such as these happen every few days, simultaneously at different places across the town. Much bigger protests, hundreds of thousands strong, take place in remembrance of Neda Agha-Soltan and the other martyrs of June 20, and again on July 15, when Rafsanjani delivers a pro-Mousavi sermon at Friday Prayers. Each protest is a blow to the hardliners and a victory for the opposition, but the drip-drip of arrests continues and there is ominously little word from hundreds of detainees.

The *Basij* deploy their forces and there is a baton charge or some pepper-gas canisters are fired. The marchers scatter like birds. A few demonstrators are arrested. The others gather again. At the centre of the movement are those young men who engage in running battles with the *basijis* and riot police. Female protesters become logisticians. They keep up a supply of bricks and tiles from a nearby building site. You come across some surprising women doing this, including some of the older ones. They say, 'You can't fight guns with words!'

Fluidity is the key. You start in a main road. You spill into a side-street. You lope, bouncing on soft soles, past the riot police and into the embrace of 100 welcoming protesters. 'Don't be scared! We are all together!' There is an electric intensity when you defy something that, in the past, you only feared. Mohsen's throwing arm is getting stronger.

During one of the protests, walking among a group of young men, Mohsen notices that someone nearby is taking pictures of him with his cellphone. It's common enough to see protesters recording events to send abroad or to show friends, but this man's lens lingers on Mohsen's face. When the man sees that Mohsen is staring at him, he hurriedly puts his cellphone into his pocket. The man is clean-shaven and wears jeans and more expensive sneakers than Mohsen could afford. He doesn't look out of place among the Mousavi supporters. The young man tries to distance himself from Mohsen by moving forward through the crowd. Mohsen follows.

A few minutes later, thinking that Mohsen is a safe distance away, the young man takes his cellphone out of his pocket and starts taking shots of the other marchers, this time more surreptitiously. Mohsen moves alongside him and demands, 'What are you doing?' The other man replies nervously, 'I'm collecting keepsakes.' Some of the other marchers have noticed the altercation and are observing with interest. Then the young man betrays himself by glancing over at the opposite side of the road, where a group of plain-clothes goons carrying truncheons are walking in step with the protesters.

'Spy!' Mohsen shouts furiously. He snatches the man's cell-phone and scrolls through his images. 'Look! This phone is full of close-ups of all of us!' Someone else grabs the phone and a moment later it lies in smithereens on the road.

'Filth!' someone shouts, and the terrified spy careers forward, propelled from behind. Someone sticks out a leg and he falls to the ground. Five or six marchers gather around the prostrate figure, but a man shouts, 'Don't kill him! You've destroyed the phone; now let him go!' Then someone yells, 'Run!' Mohsen looks up and sees the plain-clothes men racing across the road to save their colleague. He runs with the others.

We are in a psychological war. The dictators are fighting so that terror overtakes us and we can no longer resist. We are fighting to show we are not afraid. The pro-government sites show photos of the demonstrators and ask people to identify them. The number of government agents in disguise among the protesters is rising. They are trying to create distrust and paranoia inside the movement.

Some footage is doing the rounds of a *basiji* viciously beating a woman demonstrator. The *basiji*'s name, address and place of work have been made public by people he knows, and he is forced into hiding. Protesters exchange stories of dead and injured *basijis*, *basijis* being run over by cars. A senior police officer says that 500 members of the security forces were hospitalised on June 20. He is trying to present the *basijis* as the wronged party, but they come across as losers.

Shadi gets back from a three-day trip to see her parents, up north on the Caspian Sea coast. A few days later she bumps into Mohsen after a demonstration, and together they walk home. Shadi's account makes the Chaloos Road through the Alborz Mountains sound like a huge Mousavi rally. Drivers leaning on their horns, car-loads of people flashing V-for-victory signs, motorists displaying anything green that comes to hand: cucumbers, watermelons, whole oleander bushes. Every so often squads of riot police, two to a bike, screaming down the middle of the road with their silencers off, trying to intimidate people.

'One of them came alongside my brother's car for a while,' Shadi says, 'but the man riding pillion subtly made a victory sign against the black of his beard.'

The country is in an uncertain frame of mind. The Iranians are a self-obsessed people and their belief that they are owed attention has been sharpened by recent events. But ever since the revolution their membership in the world community has been fugitive and incomplete. It is sometimes hard to relate what is happening in Iran to what is happening elsewhere. The government and parliament are at each other's throats; Ahmadinejad's appointment of a holy fool to the office of vice-president is overturned by Khamenei; are these events vital to Iranians' understanding of history, or perfectly irrelevant? Their sense of dismemberment grows when ashen clouds of dust from the Euphrates basin sweep in and settle over the city, sealing the people from the sky. The air is deadly and the authorities order children and old people to stay at home.

The fanatics have their own cosmic interpretations of the augurs. Some read the apocalyptic weather and the cracks in the revolutionary façade as signs of the natural and social anarchy that are prerequisites to the re-emergence of the Hidden Imam. According to this heresy, chaos should be welcomed; indeed, it should be actively generated. The head of the armed forces addresses a fraternal open letter to the Hidden Imam, in which he lays bare his fears for the country and accuses the protesters of turning guns of American, British and Israeli origin on their own people.

There is a second belief – that Islam's code of laws and conduct may be set aside in a conflict against the enemies of God. Perhaps this explains why the *basijis* scream profanities and brutally manhandle the women protesters. Perhaps it explains the unspeakable rumours that have started emerging from detention centres like Kahrizak – that there has been a suspension of Islamic law inside these places, and a descent to animal barbarism.

The facts seem to corroborate the rumours. A young woman activist is arrested and disappears without trace. When her parents eventually retrieve her corpse, they find that her genitals and face have been burned by acid. This is a rudimentary camouflage, an autopsy reveals, for the multiple violations that she has suffered in the course of her excruciating death. Mohsen is not alone in believing that the authorities are controlling the flow of horrendous stories, propagating the worst of them, in order to scare people.

Everything these days has a political hue. An airliner crashes on its way from Tehran to Armenia, killing all passengers. The machine is a rankly unsafe Russian Tupolev, an ancient contraption that Western countries won't let into their airspace. In the days following the crash there is an attempt to blame the pilot and make out that the plane was in perfect condition. No one buys this. Iran is prevented by sanctions from purchasing many things from the United States and Europe, and Russia has stepped in to help ease Iran's isolation. The Russians have built Iran's first nuclear reactor. They are in negotiations to sell Iran a missile defence system. They have made millions by selling Iran dozens of crappy airliners.

The more they think about Russia's alliance with the Islamic Republic, the more the people find that it stinks. The Russians use their status as a permanent member of the United Nations Security Council to prevent the imposition of effective sanctions against the Islamic Republic. The people won't easily forget the image of a grinning Medvedev welcoming Ahmadinejad to Moscow immediately after the stolen election. Rumours continue to fly of Russia's role in training Iran in the finer points of crowd control and repression, just as the Israelis and Americans did before the revolution. Now, after 'Allahu Akbar' and 'Death to the Dictator', the people shout, 'Death to Russia!'

A few days later it's China's turn. The Chinese are butchering their Muslims in the province of Sinkiang, but Iranian officialdom studiously looks the other way, for China, like Russia, has a strategic alliance with the Islamic Republic. China buys Iranian hydrocarbons and Iran's internal markets are awash with Chinese goods. The reticence of Khamenei, Ahmadinejad and the others is striking when you consider their aggressive championing of the Palestinian cause and their self-depiction as defenders of Muslims everywhere. The same men, of course, stayed obligingly silent while Russia massacred the Chechens.

Life between the protests is made up of hearsay and subversion and self-fulfilling prophecies. The SMS service is restored. The movement responds: boycott SMSs! That will cost the telecoms company a packet! One morning there is green paint running down the street; after lunch the street cleaners are down on their knees, swearing under their breath. It's rumoured that the authorities intend to use swine flu as a pretext to keep schools and universities closed when the new academic year rolls around. It's not beyond them, says Mohsen's father, remembering the Cultural Revolution of the early 1980s, when the universities were shut and a generation of teachers purged.

Shadi thinks the state has been embarrassed by the images of violence; everyone knows the Islamic Republic craves international legitimacy. Mohsen's father has a different view. 'These guys don't get embarrassed. They want everyone to see what animals they are so that the opposition gets scared.'

It's common knowledge that top officials are divided over whether state TV should broadcast confessions that prominent political prisoners have been forced to make over the past few weeks. Mohsen has heard about an earlier series of confessions by members of the Communist *Tudeh* Party, dating back twenty years. These confessions helped destroy the party's credibility and underscored, in the public eye, the superiority of political Islam over rival ideologies.

Iran has changed since then. The people, argue the opponents of televised confessions, are more cynical and savvy. Everyone would know that such confessions have been extracted under torture. They would have the opposite effect to that intended.

Ahmadinejad's decision to sack his intelligence minister, Mohseni-Ejei, may be connected to this controversy. Besides opposing the holy fool's appointment, it is thought that Mohseni-Ejei told the nation's leaders some unpalatable home truths. In a damning report, he is said to have dismissed allegations of an attempted colour revolution, advocated the demilitarisation of public life and argued strongly against public confessions. Several more senior men from the ministry go. The Intelligence Ministry is a vast, well-resourced organisation. Who controls the safe-houses now, the spooks and interrogators?

One day Mr Hojjati, the head of the residents' association in the Abbaspours' apartment building, is summoned to the local police station. According to local reports, a policeman tells him, subversive slogans have been heard from the roof of the building. If they continue, Mr Hojjati will be held responsible. Mr Hojjati enquires how it is that 'Allahu Akbar', yesterday's call for justice, has now become unacceptable. The policeman shrugs. It's not his job to explain the directives he receives.

That night, rather than gather on the rooftop, the residents of the apartment block convene in Mr Hojjati's house. Mrs Ruhani, another resident, is firm about the course she thinks should be followed. If the nightly protests continue, she says, not only will Mr Hojjati get into trouble, but there is every chance that the basijis will intervene. 'And we all know what that means,' she says ominously. The residents of the block vote to call a halt. Mohsen's father is pleased. 'Adventurers!' he says. 'Individualists!'

Mohsen has given up trying to find a new job. What is the point? No one is advertising and no one who has advertised is hiring. For the first time in his life Mohsen feels as though he is a part of something worthwhile. One day he hits a basiji for the first time, with a large piece of masonry. That's a tendon, he thinks as the basiji drops to his knees and a fountain of blood sprays from his shoulder. Later on he tells Shadi. Not long ago she would have been furious. Now she feels a thrill of satisfaction whenever she hears that a basiji has been hurt.

Mohsen sees a lot of the same faces at the protests. Everyone knows each other, though they don't tell each other their names. Mohsen is far from being the most reckless or brave of the protesters, but he is good at gestures. One day he jumps on top of a stationary car and rips open his shirt to reveal a green

T-shirt underneath. Then he unties the strip from around his neck and unfurls Shamlu's words against the sky.

The next day his photograph is posted on one of the sites. He is handsome with his green mask and dark, intense eyes. He thinks of Solmaz, bent over her books, and wonders if she has seen the photograph and guessed who the dashing freedom-fighter is.

It is August 5, the day when Ahmadinejad is to be sworn in as Iran's re-elected president. Everyone knows the security forces will be out in strength, but thousands of opposition activists take to the streets anyway. It was to stop this day that the movement was set in motion all those weeks ago. If it cannot be stopped, at least it will be spoiled.

It's a boiling hot summer's day. A north-westerly wind has blown away the dust. The streets all around are packed with uniformed *basijis*, plain-clothes goons, regular policemen and riot police. The protesters wander nervously in small groups. The security forces rush them whenever they stop or try to join other groups. Some of the protesters worry it's a trap – that they're being moved on to a specific location where they can be attacked.

Mohsen finds a small group of demonstrators to join. He recognises none of them. They shout, 'Neda didn't die; this regime died!' They shout, 'Our Leader's a killer and his rule is defunct!' Some cops stand on the other side of the road. Mohsen turns to the man marching next to him and says, 'They don't want bloodshed today, of all days.' The man smiles grimly and replies, 'they want bloodshed, whatever the day!'

Mohsen sees a protester sprinting towards them, whooping and laughing. He's a tall young man and he's being pursued by a stout *basiji*, who is pink with rage. The protesters open their ranks to let the protester through. Then they close up again, barring the *basiji*'s way. 'Where did he go?' demands the *basiji*, panting with fury, and the little crowd presses in around him, enjoying his discomfort. 'Where did he go?'

Mohsen can't resist a bit of fun. 'Who are you talking about?'

he asks innocently, and the other protesters snigger. The *basiji*'s eyes widen and fix on Mohsen's. He is about Mohsen's height, with an unusually fair complexion and a soft, meaty face. The *basiji* nods, studying Mohsen. He says quietly, 'Today you died', and turns back.

Some of the other protesters advise Mohsen to go home. 'He'll come back and find you,' says the same man Mohsen spoke to earlier. Someone else asks why Mohsen isn't wearing a mask, and he realises he's forgotten to bring it. He pulls his Shamlu strip up over his mouth like a kerchief, and asks someone to tighten it from the back. Now the group is walking away from the parliament building. 'I'll walk a little while,' Mohsen thinks, 'and then go home.' At the next opportunity, wherever the concentration of security forces is a little thinner, he will separate from the group.

Suddenly Mohsen feels an excruciating pain in his back. A split-second later he is face-down on the sidewalk, unable to move. He sees the backs of the protesters, running away. One man has turned to look at him. He shouts, 'Leave him alone!' But the man's companion grabs his arm and he starts running again. Then Mohsen's face is smashed into the concrete pavement and his arms are yanked from behind and he thinks his wrists are going to break. He receives a second blow on the back. The cuffs bite into his skin. Never before has he experienced such pain. Someone shouts, 'Get him into the van!'

Mohsen is dragged to his feet and propelled across the road. The van is in a side-street. Its back doors are open and it's empty. A plain-clothes *basiji* runs over to Mohsen, blindfolds him and bundles him into the van. The van doors are shut and immediately the truncheon blows start – on his back, ribs, ankles and arms. The truncheon is striking the roof and sides of the van as his assailant draws it back. Mohsen dimly wonders if it's the same meaty-faced *basiji*, carrying out his threat to kill him. Suddenly the doors of the van are drawn open and an older voice snaps, 'Get this lot blindfolded and cuffed and inside!' Mohsen's assailant shoves him up to the far end of the van and orders him to sit cross-legged on the floor. Other people are being bundled in. They shuffle as far up as they can and sit down. 'No talking!' comes the older voice.

The van drives off. Mohsen and the others press involuntarily against each another whenever the van goes around a corner, and the man next to Mohsen groans softly. The van crosses a bridge. Now it strains up a hill. The older voice speaks into a walkie-talkie. He tells the other person that there are ten in the van and that he's making tracks towards the destination. A little further on the van stops and one of the men up front curses and Mohsen can hear slogans in the street outside. For one moment he thinks the protesters are going to liberate them all, but then the van swerves away from the noise and into a quiet street. A little further on it stops. Someone standing in the street is talking to the driver. 'You should be fine if you take the normal route, but don't come off the freeway or you'll get caught up in the crowd.'

One of the detainees in the van is whispering. Someone barks, 'No talking!' He goes on, ironically, 'This time will be different from all the other times. We've got something special lined up for you.'

The van stops, the engine cuts out. The doors open again and another assault begins. The prisoners are pulled out of the back of the van. The swearing resumes. A hand grabs Mohsen's collar and pulls him out. He falls heavily onto a hot, hard, paved surface. 'Get up, trash!' He is slammed into the side of the van. There's a shout. 'We need these cuffs! Get them off and put them back in the van!' Someone unlocks Mohsen's cuffs. His wrists are bloody and raw. Then he is being propelled very fast, like an animal, under the sun. The man pushing him is cursing non-stop.

Mohsen is shoved indoors. It smells of sweat and urine and, overlying these smells, something else, unspeakable and rancid. Now Mohsen is being pushed with more care, apparently by someone else, but as he walks his feet hit the bodies of men on the floor, eliciting grunts. He must be in a corridor between two lines of cells. He is being guided in a straight line and can hear snatches of conversation from both sides as he passes. They descend a flight of metal steps and double back on themselves and then they're in another corridor. They come to a halt and the man orders Mohsen to give him everything he has in his pockets. Mohsen is carrying his keys and some money. 'No ID, eh? What about your phone?' Giving Mohsen a shove, he says, 'Sit in there and don't take off your blindfold!' Mohsen sits with his back leaning against a wall. He hears footsteps as the man goes away.

Mohsen is in a cell with several other people. Some of them are conversing softly. One of them is saying a prayer in Arabic. He also hears the voices of prisoners from the other cells, and from the corridor outside. There are shouts for water and the curses of the warders, and occasionally a cry of pain when someone is hit. Every now and then there is a commotion and someone is dragged down the corridor and shoved into an open cell. Mohsen sweats profusely from the intense heat.

Later, Mohsen's first hours of incarceration will assume a disproportionate, nostalgic importance, not only because their physical discomforts – a claw in his back, a throbbing tooth – will seem comparatively inconsequential, but because his experiences are readily comprehensible. He guesses that he's in Evin Prison and he hears the other detainees around him and is reassured by their presence. In a short time, however, the combined effects of physical deterioration, his mental torments and his blindfold will confuse Mohsen's understanding of where he is, and this, in turn, will confuse his understanding of time – to the extent that, when he is eventually released from captivity, he will have little idea how long he was inside, and it will not matter to him.

For the moment Mohsen has the luxuries of terror and deliberation. He has heard of men who resist in jail and of others who squeal. Over the past few weeks, thinking idly about arrest and torture, he has wondered which of these categories he would fall into. He imagines being treated as one of the tricky, important prisoners – a nut to be cracked. He is no *lumpen*.

He has read the reformist tracts and has some knowledge of philosophy. Above all he is afraid that he will find himself being interrogated by the man in the white shirt.

In reality Mohsen doesn't occupy such a privileged position. He's not one of those imprisoned reformists one reads about in the papers. He might easily not have been arrested today; he might now be sitting at home, having tea with his mother or cramming the last of his possessions into his bag before heading off to Greece. Mohsen's fate hasn't been written anywhere because he's not important enough. In common with the vast majority of people who languish in the regime's detention centres, he's like a piece of driftwood on the surface of the sea, and it will be a matter of luck as to whether he'll be washed up on the shore or swept out by the ebb-tide.

Mohsen is starting to feel thirsty when a voice next to him whispers, 'Where were you?' Mohsen tells the voice where he was at the time of his arrest, and poses the same question in response. It emerges that they were close to each other; the voice was arrested an hour or two before Mohsen. They speak for a few moments about things outside and Mohsen asks the voice if he has been given anything to eat or drink, to which he replies that he has not. 'They won't give us anything until day two,' the voice says, 'that is, assuming we stay that long. I don't think they'll keep many of us here. This is only a sorting centre.' He goes on, more softly, 'Be careful what you say. They bug the cells and they may have cameras too.'

A warder is walking in the corridor. 'No talking!' he shouts. He starts to shout something else, but stops himself because another man has started speaking, evenly but at a deafening volume. The man's voice is coming from loudspeakers, and it takes Mohsen several seconds to realise that he has heard this speech before. It's the speech Khamenei made a few days ago when he officially appointed Ahmadinejad to be president. Mohsen heard it on the evening news, after he got back from the demonstration.

After Khamenei has finished, the loudspeakers blast out a

confession by a man whose voice is calm and heavy, as if he has sat in a Turkish bath for a long time and feels pleasantly drained. This man doesn't introduce himself, but he gives the impression that he is on intimate terms with the top reformists, who, he says, hatched a plot conceived in London to launch a velvet revolution. It's an intricate plot, involving NGOs and the Voice of America and BBC Persian, and the man speaking is only sorry that he and many others were deceived by certain politicians into playing into the hands of the counter-revolutionaries. The confession stops as abruptly as it began.

Mohsen doesn't know how long it is before he wakes from an uneasy sleep to find his tooth throbbing and hunger coiled in his belly. A man is shouting from above him, 'Get up!' The man grips him by the arm and Mohsen hauls himself to his feet. He is propelled out of the cell and into the corridor. Mohsen is now vividly, helplessly awake. He is being taken away from the packed corridor and away from the voice, his friend.

At the end of a long, winding journey Mohsen's blindfold is removed. The warder says, 'Write!' and goes out, slamming the door. Mohsen's eyes get used to his new surroundings. If anything, this cell is even hotter than the previous one, but it is relatively clean and there is no dreadful smell. Through the bars on the small window he can see down into a small yard. Mohsen is on the second floor, but he has no recollection of climbing steps. And the sun is near its zenith. Has he just arrived at Evin, or has a whole day passed since his arrest? There is a metal chair and desk, and on the desk a ballpoint pen and some sheets of paper with questions in longhand written on them.

Mohsen is grateful for the distraction afforded by the questionnaire. It's reassuring to write down who he is and where he lives, his father's name and profession, and the schools he attended. Later on the questionnaire becomes political. Were you active on behalf of any of the presidential candidates? Which one? Mohsen describes how he joined the Mousavi camp, his campaigning activities, and the protests he attended after the election results. He doesn't deny attending the protests, but gives a negative response to the question 'Did you engage in hostile actions towards the security forces or participate in the vandalism of public or private property?'

Near the end of the questionnaire he is asked to describe in as much detail as possible his colleagues in the campaign team. Did they express an opinion regarding the Guardianship of the Jurist? What contacts did they have with foreigners? Did he ever hear them speak favourably of President Obama? This section is trickier and on several occasions Mohsen replies, 'I do not know this person well enough to be able to answer the question.' With respect to foreigners, so far as he knows, no one in the campaign team had any such contacts – unless you count an interview that the Doctor gave an Italian journalist shortly before the election. Mohsen describes this interview because it reflects well on the Doctor. The Doctor strenuously objected when the journalist suggested that Mousavi's ultimate objective was to abolish the Islamic Republic.

When Mohsen finishes answering the questionnaire he feels more optimistic. The detention centres must be full to bursting, the authorities looking for excuses to let people go. Mohsen convinces himself that his questionnaire is a strong argument for his release. As instructed, he places it in the hatch that is used for passing things in and out of the cell. Half an hour later the papers are gone and in their place are some stale bread and a bowl of watery soup. Mohsen gobbles down his food, but there is something in it that makes him feel heavy and tired. He is falling into an uneasy sleep, sitting on the metal chair, when a different warder appears, cuffs him and says, 'Get up.'

Mohsen is back in his old cell – or one very like it. He has stomach-cramps from the food, and the painkillers the warder gave him for his tooth have had little effect. Inside the cells, the no-talking rule is strictly enforced. Once a day the prisoners are taken in groups of four to a foul-smelling toilet, where their cuffs and blindfolds are removed. Mohsen has been able to wash the blood off his wrists. Other than that, the detainees must remain immobile.

He hears snatches of the prayers being spoken around him

and wonders whether he should whisper prayers of his own, addressing the only God he can stomach, that of the mystic poets. Piously he decides not. He is still sufficiently the old godless Mohsen; he will not call on a God he has rejected because he lies in Evin Prison, but will face whatever is to come like the rationalist he is.

One of Mohsen's fellow inmates shits himself. The other inmates bang on the cell door and shout for water, which enrages the warders, who come in and beat everyone with lengths of electric cable. They particularly beat the prisoner in question, who shits himself again.

When they eventually come for Mohsen, there is something in the way he is propelled, in the curses to which he is subjected, that strikes him as a terrible omen. Mohsen almost allows himself to drop to his knees as he walks, to implore God, to implore Mr Khamenei, but he knows he'll be beaten all the worse if he does. This walk along the corridors, this sense he has of being a sheep going to slaughter, will be the last prison memory he can evoke without breaking down.

Mohsen is taken into a room where two men are chatting amicably about cars. One of these men, whose voice is quick and squeaky, does most of the talking. There is a second man, gruffer, taciturn. The two men carry on speaking after Mohsen has been brought before them and left there. Then, without warning, the conversation stops.

In no time the gruff one is in a fury. 'You have five minutes to save yourself,' he says, 'though I think five minutes is excessive, considering the insulting replies you gave to our questions.' Astonished, Mohsen opens his mouth to reply when he receives a slap hard enough to daze him. 'Let me ask you this,' the interrogator goes on. 'Do you think our questions were framed disrespectfully? Is that why you replied as you did?'

Mohsen shakes his head vigorously. 'No! Not at all! How did you find my answers insulting? This is surely a misunderstanding . . .'

A fist drives into Mohsen's solar plexus and the same man, breathing more heavily, goes on, 'Did you really think you could fool us by making out you didn't know the others in the campaign, or were you simply showing us your contempt?' Mohsen is fighting for breath. The voice goes on, 'Is it possible for us, who know the depths of Mr Mousavi's betrayal, and the betrayal committed by his supporters across this city – is it possible for us to enjoy your banal story about an Italian journalist? Did you not anticipate that we would find these answers impertinent?'

The high-pitched one says, 'I think this person is irredeemable! I doubt he can be turned into a man!'

Mohsen pleads, 'In the name of God, just tell me how I . . .' He receives another blow, this one on the nose, and his eyes fill with tears.

'You dare invoke God?' the gruff one goes on. 'You're unclean and have declared war on God and the Hidden Imam, and yet you invoke His name?'

Mohsen is trying to save himself. 'If you could only tell me . . . perhaps ask me questions. Perhaps I've become confused in here, forgotten things . . .'

'We don't need your information,' the high-pitched one interrupts. 'We already know everything. The important thing is that you appreciate the seriousness of what you have done wrong. My fear is that you have been so polluted, you're not even aware of what you do. And that makes you doubly dangerous for society. This is what we're trying to find out. We're doing this because we want to save you.'

The gruff one sighs. 'Shall we give him one more chance? I think we can give him one more chance.' He tells Mohsen the story of the Shia Imam who once condemned an innocent man to death for murder. 'Just before the man's execution, the real killer came forward and the Imam ordered that his life be spared as he had saved the government from carrying out an unlawful killing.' If he is frank and honest, the gruff one is saying, Mohsen can count on merciful treatment.

Mohsen is sat down on a metal chair. Papers are shuffled. The gruff one asks the questions. He asks about the Doctor, Shadi and Pegah. Mohsen referred to all three in his original answers, without writing anything incriminatory. Now he wants Mohsen to talk about Shadi's and Pegah's membership of the One Million Signatures Campaign. What happened when the Doctor visited Dubai last summer? What did he discuss when he met with an officer from the US consulate there?

Mohsen knows little about these things, but to admit this would be fatal. Instead he tells them that Shadi has contacts in an American NGO that monitors human rights in Iran, and that she has been publicising the Doctor's case through them. He recounts the time when Pegah said as a joke, 'If only the Americans would come and invade us, now they're done with Iraq and Afghanistan!' Mohsen hears the scratch of a pencil on the page, and he feels relieved. He would say anything to keep them writing, to take their minds off hurting him.

Mohsen has an idea. He requests a piece of paper and a pencil and asks that his blindfold and cuffs be taken off for a few minutes. The high-pitched one says smoothly, 'Tell me whatever it is you want to write down, and I'll write it for you.'

Mohsen composes himself and says, 'I would like to say how sorry I am that I disregarded the advice of the Supreme Leader when he ordered us to desist from further protests. I regret this act of selfishness and disobedience, and am prepared to do anything to safeguard the Islamic Republic and its achievements against our foreign enemies.'

Mohsen has barely finished speaking when he is knocked to the floor by a furious volley of blows. The gruff one says harshly, 'Empty displays of penitence are worthless to us! You must confess fully before you are in a position to regret. It's not enough to surrender on the outside. Your surrender must be internal.' His next comment is directed at his colleague. 'You know, I think you may be right, and he will never become a man.'

But Mohsen can confess no more. He doesn't know the nature of the relationship between the Doctor and the sister of a senior reformist. When the gruff one mentions a certain meeting that Pegah had with a human-rights specialist based in Belgium, Mohsen pretends to have heard about this, only to get hit again.

The meeting never took place. They are trying to catch him out. Mohsen volunteers that he was once refused a visa to Italy. His interrogators stay silent.

The sky is turning black above Mohsen. He fumbles for something, anything, to incriminate Pegah. 'She has a sister who has been given refugee status in Brussels!' Mohsen can't figure out what his interrogators are trying to achieve. Is it possible that they know something he doesn't, or are they simply trying to get him to incriminate his friends? 'If only you would jog my memory,' he pleads, 'you'll find me helpful and accommodating.'

At length Mohsen hears the papers being shuffled again. The gruff one says in a matter-of-fact voice, 'You have disappointed me. You have made me look foolish in front of my colleague. You have not shown any desire to save yourself, which can only mean you are stupid. Above all, when I read your answers to our guileless questions, I see that you have underestimated us. We are simple men, yes, with a simple faith, but we know certain things. Do we not know who is throwing bricks at the forces of law and order in Shariati Street on a particular day? Do we not know who is shouting, "Death to Khamenei"?' He clears his throat. 'We have given you a chance to reflect on your actions and draw the appropriate conclusions. We presumed you were wise enough to see the error of your ways. We gave you gold, my friend. And you spat in our faces.'

There is a silence.

'I am left with no option,' the gruff one goes on, 'but to concur with my colleague here. He believes that you are a common hooligan, and he has been proved right. From now on, this is how you will be treated.'

There is the sound of scraping chairs and the two men rise to their feet. In his panic Mohsen also tries to get up, but a heavy hand presses down on his shoulder. Mohsen realises that the hand belongs to a third person, who has been motionless up till now. The cell-door slams shut and Mohsen sits again, dully. The third person is unlocking his cuffs. For a moment, Mohsen thinks it was all a joke. He is about to be freed.

Suddenly Mohsen finds himself being lifted up and hurled face-down onto a metal bed. His socks are being yanked off his feet. His right hand is cuffed to the top of the bed and ropes are tied around his ankles, pulled fast and knotted somewhere below. He pleads, 'O God . . .'

'Don't expect God to help you!' the new voice taunts. 'You should try, "O Bush! O Obama! O Netanyahu!"' The voice is coming from the foot of the bed. The man intones, 'In the Name of God, the Merciful, the Compassionate . . .' Mohsen braces himself.

There is a terse whisper and the instrument comes crashing onto the soles of Mohsen's feet. An unimaginable pain shoots through his body to his temples, a pain to drive one mad. Mohsen is dimly aware that he is screaming. His wrist and ankles are being cut up as he thrashes against his bonds.

The beating continues. Before each blow, the man calls, 'Ya! Hossein!' After a while he stops to catch his breath. He speaks to Mohsen. He calls him a Hypocrite and a traitor to God. Then he starts again.

It lasts for ever. The pain doesn't get better as it goes on. It gets deeper. By the end Mohsen hears things only in bits. He is groaning and expecting the next blow and he doesn't realise that his bonds have been undone and his tormentor has left the cell. He lies there for a long time, overcome.

By the time the warder comes in, Mohsen's agony has subsided a little. The pain is concentrated in his feet and there's another discomfort: he needs to urinate. 'Get up and try to walk,' says the warder. 'It's the only way to stop the swelling.' He takes Mohsen under his armpit and heaves him up. Mohsen is terrified that if he pisses himself he will get beaten again.

The warder helps Mohsen out of the cell and down the corridor. Mohsen walks like a drunkard because of his ragged soles. The warder loosens his blindfold and Mohsen takes it off before he enters the toilet. He follows the warder's advice by balming his feet under the tap, low on the wall, that is used for filling ewers. From outside the toilet the warder says, 'Don't be tempted to have a drink. It'll play havoc with your kidneys.'

Back in the cell, the warder tells Mohsen to stand with his back against the wall and to go up and down on the balls of his feet. Later he brings him tea with lots of sugar in it. Lying on the bed, it occurs to him that the warder has been sympathetic to him. 'Of course they want the swelling to go down!' he says to himself. 'That way they can beat me again!'

A couple of days later Mohsen is transferred.

Mohsen remembers being driven in a van and he knows he won't be freed because the warder back at Evin has told him he's going somewhere worse. They arrive somewhere and they throw him out of the van and he hits something and falls onto the ground. They play with him, make him walk into a tree. Then they pour gasoline over him and one of them says, 'Light the match!' and they laugh. They make him stand in the sun for a long time and the gasoline vaporises and it feels like the skin is burning off his body.

They throw him into an industrial container full of other living corpses, stinking of piss, boiling hot. Lunch is bread and water and sometimes a potato or two. Or maybe this is breakfast – the days are elastic in the container. One of the warders makes them bark like dogs to get their food. Another gives them water out of a gasoline drum, which makes them gag.

Every now and then they take away certain prisoners for special treatment. The lucky ones are only beaten. Some have their hands put in burning hot tar. Some are hung up by their wrists or ankles. One comes back stinking of shit. They forced his face into a blocked toilet until the filth entered his throat through his nose.

Once or twice a day they come in and beat everyone with fan belts and lengths of cable. 'We'll show you what a velvet revolution is!' Wrists and ankles and teeth, all broken. Mohsen's blindfold slips and he sees the people beating him and it strikes him how ordinary they look.

Every so often – the sound of a helicopter. He hears the helicopters at night, even now, in his sleep.

The interrogations aren't really interrogations. The prisoners haven't been brought here to tell. They've been brought here to learn some manners.

One says, 'How long is it since you last fucked a woman? Don't worry. I'm not like the others, trying to ram their pricks inside you!' This place, he goes on, is where the drug addicts and pimps get taken, and no one gives a damn about them. Why does Obama care so much about you, but not about the dealers and pimps?

At night the prisoners sleep on the feet and legs of the next prisoner.

The door is flung open. 'You! The pretty one!' They hurl him into a room. 'Stay here and someone will come along and give you one.' He scrabbles around on the floor. Nothing sharp to slit his wrists with. He gets down and prays. Someone comes in and yanks him to his feet and tells him to run. 'Faster!' He runs and hits the wall and breaks his nose. 'Queer boy! Can't you tell where the wall is?' Again, run. Fall down. He sleeps, perhaps, and then they come and take him away again.

Another voice: 'Take care of him for half an hour until I come back.' He's beaten again. 'We're only giving you back your vote. Isn't that what you wanted?' Another warden, a mild-voiced one, tells him, 'Everyone must leave the world at his allotted time, and there is always someone waiting to take his place.'

He's taken to a different room. 'Go and impregnate him! Teach him a lesson!'

He begs. He cries. He says, 'Aren't you Muslims?'

They say, 'Anything we do to you – anything at all – is considered an act of worship. Fucking you is a good deed in the eyes of God.'

Tied down as for a bastinado. The heavy man on top, panting. 'Here! Have your vote back.'

He loses consciousness from the pain. He is dead.

Back in a different cell. All like him. No blindfolds in here. The floor is covered in blood and flies. They do it to them once a day, sometimes twice. They take them out and do it, and then they bring them back in again. They give them drugs to make them sleep. Every day, how many days he can't remember. One day he's so bad . . . you don't need the details.

One day he wakes up with one hand attached to a drip and another chained to the bedhead. They sew him up. 'You'll be out in a couple of days. We need the bed.'

They give him a shower and get him to sign a bit of paper saying he's been well treated in jail and promising not to take part in another demonstration. They say he'll be informed of any charges later on.

In his room in the Abbaspours' apartment, Mohsen sits with Shadi in silence. They sit and then his face grows troubled and he wants to say something else, perhaps the most painful thing of all, but again his throat won't let him. Shadi tries to soothe him, calm him, but this only makes him more agitated.

Finally, a supreme effort, he forces it out. He spoke about her and the others in Evin, he betrayed them. He betrayed them all. He's not a man any more. He's nothing.

6

The summer ended, but the Islamic Republic lived on. The West started fresh negotiations with Iran about its nuclear programme. The Iranians tested a ballistic missile, and dozens of Tehran's schools were strengthened against a possible earthquake. The universities reopened. The campuses were full of spies and informants.

The Islamic Republic mounted a huge show trial. Dozens of hours' worth of recantations were read out by leading reformists, Iranians working for foreign embassies, and 'rioters' no one had heard of. Some of the nonentities were sentenced to death, but the prominent reformists got lesser sentences because the authorities had decided to avoid provocative gestures that might reignite the movement. Some of the reformists were freed on bail pending appeal. The authorities secured their silence by threatening them or by demanding huge bail sureties.

The people watched episodes from the trial on television. They saw people they knew, former top officials, sitting stunned and emaciated in prison uniform. These people confessed to falling into the trap set by foreigners and participating in a grand conspiracy. These people ridiculed the absurd notion that anyone but Ahmadinejad had won the election. They dished the dirt on Mousavi, on Rafsanjani and his children, and on the foreign embassies that had encouraged the protesters and given refuge to the injured rioters. They expressed chagrin at their own stupidity and requested forgiveness and understanding. Some of these people spoke of their crimes with unnatural briskness, even levity, as if they were remembering the misdemeanours of someone they barely knew.

Others did not speak. They sat watching the proceedings, and Tehran was rife with rumours that these people had refused to buckle, despite suffering horrendously, and their prestige rose.

The demonstrations fell in number and intensity. A gap opened between Mousavi and Karrubi on the one hand, who continued to assert their loyalty to the Islamic Republic, and their more radical followers, on the other. During the demonstrations some people stamped on pictures of the Supreme Leader. Khamenei allowed some criticism of himself to be broadcast on TV. This was designed to illustrate his strength and confidence. In fact it showed the opposite. On December 7, universities around the country erupted in further protests.

Iran's nuclear negotiations with the US and Europe ended amid mutual recrimination. The US signalled its intention to press for stronger sanctions against Iran at the United Nations Security Council. The pundits speculated that the likelihood of military strikes on Iran, either by Israel or the United States, was increasing by the day.

The Islamic Republic entered the last and perhaps dirtiest phase of its life, a phase of fear and sordidness, theft and fantasy. How long it will last, no one knows, but there is no prospect of regime-saving reform, no sign of a great leader to bring the country out of the morass, no balm to heal the wounds. Things will get better, the people say, but only after they have gotten worse.

Six weeks after his release Mohsen Abbaspour went to see the taxi-driver who had brought him home. He wanted to return the taxi-driver's clothes. The taxi-driver and his wife, a petite, chador-clad woman, invited Mohsen in for tea, and they asked him what he planned to do. Mohsen mentioned that he was contemplating joining a friend of his who had slipped into Europe and was working there. The taxi-driver nodded and said, 'You look as though you could do with a change of air.' Then he asked, 'Aren't you barred from leaving the country?'

Mohsen replied, 'Not as far as I know. What do they have to gain from keeping people like me in Iran?' He shrugged. 'To be honest, I haven't decided anything yet.'

As Mohsen was leaving, the taxi-driver rested a hand on his shoulder. 'You know,' he said, 'I should tell you something. A few days before the election my wife and I had a conversation about it with my brother-in-law, and he told me that if a reformist was elected we could say goodbye to Islam and morality and safety for our children. We believed him and voted for Ahmadinejad. But that morning – the morning when I met you – I learned a lot.'

His wife corrected him. 'We both learned a lot.'

'That morning,' the taxi-driver went on, 'I went three times around the roundabout before picking you up. You were standing unsteadily on the kerb, and at first I thought you must be a bum or an addict. Something made me go around a second time – something decent in your face, I think – and then I saw the bruises on your face and the cuts on your arms and I knew these weren't bruises and cuts from some fight or other.

'We'd heard rumours about the detention centres, but my brother-in-law had said these were lies, spread by counter-revolutionaries, and my wife and I had believed him. Now, going round the roundabout for the third time, it was as if I saw the whole of the last thirty years of my life. I saw the Imam Khomeini and the war, and my love for the revolution. I knew that if I stopped I would have to face the possibility that I had lived with a lie. On the other hand, if I didn't stop, it would mean I hadn't done my duty as a human being next to God, and isn't that more important?'

His wife nodded supportively.

'So I stopped,' the taxi-driver sighed, 'and you sort of fell into the car, and I asked you where you wanted to go and you didn't answer, and I looked at you and saw you'd fallen asleep. That's why I brought you here.'

'We have a son your age,' the taxi-driver's wife said suddenly. 'He's away doing his military service.'

'Anyway,' the taxi-driver went on, 'that night, after I dropped you at your house, I came back home and I sat up with my wife and we prayed. You know, Mr Abbaspour, for us Islam is everything, and it provides the answers to all our needs. I turned to my wife and I said, "How can it be? How can it be that a government that says it's from Islam and God behaves like the devil?"

'And you know what she told me, Mr Abbaspour?' the taxi-driver went on. 'She told me a ruler cannot rule unless he is righteous. Now we have a different situation. There is no one standing over us to guide us and tell us what to do. We only have the good in our hearts to guide our decisions. We are alone, but we are free.'